D0959213

DAVID LETTERMAN'S

New Book of

TOP TEN LISTS

and

WEDDING DRESS PATTERNS FOR THE HUSKY BRIDE

DAVID LETTERMAN'S

New Book of

TOP TEN LISTS

and

WEDDING DRESS PATTERNS FOR THE HUSKY BRIDE

by

David Letterman
Steve O'Donnell

Jon Beckerman • Rob Burnett • Donick Cary
Jill Davis • Davey DiGiorgio • Dave Drabik
Alex Gregory •Matt Harrigan • Mark Hentemann
Pete Huyck • Larry Jacobson • Jeff Judah
Tim Long • Gerard Mulligan • Rodney Rothman
Bill Scheft • Cliff Schoenberg • Steve Sherrill
Joe Toplyn • Rob Young • Steve Young

BANTAM BOOKS
New York   Toronto   London   Sydney   Auckland

David Letterman's New Book of Top Ten Lists
and Wedding Dress Patterns for the Husky Bride
A Bantam Book / November 1996

BOOK DESIGN BY GLEN M. EDELSTEIN

Library of Congress Cataloging-in-Publication Data
Letterman, David.
David Letterman's new book of top ten lists and wedding dress patterns
for the husky bride / by David Letterman,
Steve O'Donnell : Jon Beckerman . . . [et al.].
p.   cm.
ISBN 0-553-10243-5
1. American wit and humor.   2. Celebrities—Humor.   3. Quotations.
I. O'Donnell, Steve.   II. Title.
PN6162.L378   1996
818′.5402—dc20   96-32909
CIP

Published simultaneously in the United States and Canada

Bantam Books are published by Bantam Books, a division of Bantam Doubleday
Dell Publishing Group, Inc. Its trademark, consisting of the words "Bantam
Books" and the portrayal of a rooster, is Registered in U.S. Patent and Trade-
mark Office and in other countries. Marca Registrada. Bantam Books, 1540
Broadway, New York, New York 10036.

PRINTED IN THE UNITED STATES OF AMERICA
BVG   10   9   8   7   6   5   4   3   2   1

ACKNOWLEDGMENTS

Thanks to:
Irwyn Applebaum
Doug Mitchell
Maria Pope
Jill Leiderman
Walter Kim
Susan Hum & Bonnie Barrett
Ken Willis & Kendall Nisbett
Spike Feresten & Louis C.K.

and George Edward Doty IV, who didn't do a damn thing to help but did ask very nicely to be mentioned in the acknowledgments.

Special thanks to the mayor and citizens of Provo, Utah, who for six long weeks allowed us to convert their town square into Dave's Chocolate Candy Land. We regret that the sequence was not used in the book after all.

PREFACE

The otter whose colorful antics fill the pages of this book really did live in our great Pacific Northwest, and he was every bit the character these stories make him out to be! I know, because the boy who found him, nursed him back to health, and freed him again was me. I dedicate this book to "Larry," a truly remarkable otter and my best friend.

Dave Letterman

INTRODUCTION

"The Top Ten List! A lighthearted bit of fluff that distracts us nightly from our cares and woes with its comical countdown of society's flaws and foibles."

That's how no less a personage than UN Secretary General Boutros Boutros-Ghali recently described the Top Ten List in a dream I had. The glow of pride I felt in his distinguished endorsement lingered for minutes after I'd awakened.

For you, the home viewer, the list is a simple, easy-to-enjoy broadcast tradition along the lines of *The Wizard of Oz* or a hockey fight. Yet this was not always the case, for the Top Ten List has "come a long way, baby," as the kids of today say.

The very first Top Ten List was discovered in 1985 under a shallow pile of leaves near the Croton Reservoir by a hiker whose name has been lost to history, though we still have his address in Peekskill, so I suppose we could find out his name if we really had to. At his mother's urging, he sent the list in to David Letterman, who at that time hosted a television program called *I'll Read Out Loud Whatever You Send In*. Letterman read the list sent in by the hiker out loud.

The public response to the new "Top Ten List" was instantaneous. Fortunately, the staggering number of complaints and threats were kept from Mr. Letterman and the feature was repeated again and again. Some even say again and again and again.

Many years have passed, but the zeal of Dave and his staff for their precious decagimmick has not diminished an iota. Each and every list continues to be painstakingly assembled and lavished with loving care. Like a dedicated gymnast, Letterman spends long hours daily practicing the unusual "backward counting" on which every Top Ten List is based. The pressure is intense, as Letterman must "unlearn" everything he has previously been taught about conventional counting. But the on-air results speak for themselves.

Behind the seamless presentation of the list stands an unsung army of technicians and stagehands, many of them pumping titanic invisible clouds of *biphenate polyseconal* into the Ed Sullivan Theatre. By the time Letterman reads the Top Ten, audience members are usually in a receptive mood. Fewer than one in a hundred develops the skin rash.

What does the future hold for the Top Ten Lists? The sky's the limit! Or should I say *the ocean*? For even as you read this page, vast farmlands on the seafloor are being cultivated in hopes that they might produce a cheap, neverending supply of lists for years to come.

"Exciting stuff!" as our nation's president frequently remarks to Dave Letterman in my passing reveries.

Hope you agree!

Steve O'Donnell
Curator, The Top Ten Museum
and Go-Cart Track
Lake George, New York

TOP TEN SIGNS YOUR SPOUSE IS HAVING AN AFFAIR BY COMPUTER

10. Lately, she sits at the computer naked

9. After signing off, he always has a cigarette

8. The giant rubber inflatable disk drive

7. In the morning, the computer screen is all fogged up

6. He's gotten amazingly good at typing with one hand

5. Every day, Bill Gates sends $10 million worth of flowers

4. The jam in the laser printer is a pair of underpants

3. During sex, she screams, *"A colon backslash enter insert!"*

2. The fax file is filled with pictures of some guy's ass

1. Lipstick on the mouse

TOP TEN EUPHEMISMS FOR "RAT" ON NEW YORK CITY MENUS

10. Wingless Squab

9. Subway Rabbit

8. Pied Piper Pot Pie

7. Times Square Longhorn

6. Squeaky Goulash

5. Longtailed Teriyaki

4. Health Inspector's Surprise

3. Bubonic Beef

2. Jumbo Mouse

1. Peach Cobbler

TOP TEN PROJECTS ON DAVID LETTERMAN'S "TO DO" LIST

10. Pull snowblower out of swimming pool

9. Combine love of bass fishing and exercise into new sport: *Bassercize!*

8. Work up courage to wear dreadlock toupee in public

7. Expand model railroad from laundry room into every room in the house

6. Call a couple of local zoos; look into getting pet monkey laid

5. Find out secret identity of Batman

4. Cut back to five hours a night on the Internet, *tops*

3. Correct that annoying typo in his Metallica tattoo

2. Just be the best damn father he can be to Madonna's baby

1. No more cigars in the shower

TOP TEN SIGNS YOU WON'T BE QUALIFYING FOR THE U.S. OLYMPIC TEAM

10. Keep accidentally burning your wrestling opponents with your cigarette

9. When you hear the starter's pistol, you ball up like a frightened armadillo

8. Boxing opponents get their gloves caught in your stomach

7. Whenever you enter a locker room, people automatically hand you their towels

6. The only aspect of weight lifting you have any talent for is the grunting

5. Can't fit your thighs between the parallel bars

4. Duck Duck Goose not yet an Olympic event

3. When your relay partner tries to take the baton, you shout, "Screw you—get your own damn stick!"

2. Refuse to wear a team uniform because you're paranoid somebody will steal the wallet out of your street clothes

1. When you get out of bed in the morning, you have trouble nailing the dismount

TOP TEN THINGS GEORGE WASHINGTON WOULD SAY IF HE WERE ALIVE TODAY

10. "Bob Dole? I ran against him in 1796."

9. "I remember when you could get a lapdance for only a nickel."

8. "The metal bird in the sky—why does it serve such lousy food?"

7. "I've got to share a holiday with *Lincoln*? When the hell did *that* happen?"

6. "Could we redesign the quarter and lose my double chin, please?"

5. "What's the deal with all these Starbucks Coffee places?"

4. "Hello, Smithsonian? I have a big date Saturday night. Can I get my teeth back?"

3. "I cannot tell a lie. O.J. did it."

2. "How do you think I'd look with a Rachel Cut?"

1. "O blessed Providence, I do love the *Baywatch*!"

TOP TEN NEW YORK CABDRIVER PET PEEVES

10. Idiots who slow down for red lights

9. When you drive down into a pothole and can't drive out the other side

8. Passengers who make you wait for your fare while they hold up a liquor store

7. Brake pedal, gas pedal—they look the same!

6. Stubborn bloodstains on the front grille

5. Beautiful young ladies who want you to stay in the front seat

4. Damp bills

3. Wiseguys who want to try on the turban

2. When your ass starts to look like a beaded seatcover

1. When running over a bike messenger makes you bite your tongue

TOP TEN REJECTED JAMES BOND GADGETS

10. Glove Compartment Slurpee Machine

9. Telephone Filter That Makes Caller's Voice Sound Like Harvey Fierstein

8. Pepper Grinder That Dispenses a Little Too Much Pepper

7. Aston Martin Sports Car with Dual Steering Wheels for Student Driver and Instructor

6. Gag T-shirt with Picture of Bond's Tuxedo on It

5. X-Ray Specs That Allow Wearer to Identify Fillings in Box of Chocolates

4. Stapler with Hidden Scotch Tape Dispenser

3. Underground Laboratory That Will Have Your Glasses Ready for You in About an Hour

2. Special Implants That Turn 007 into a 009, If You Know What I Mean

1. Ejector Pants

TOP TEN THINGS THAT WILL GET YOU KICKED OUT OF THE MISS AMERICA PAGEANT

10. Accidentally leaving the price tag on your breasts

9. Constantly yelling *"Gong her!"* during the talent competition

8. They look it up and find out there is no "East Dakota"

7. Three Words: Painful chronic hiccups

6. Putting Vaseline over your entire face

5. Wearing a sash that says FUCK YOU

4. Your talent? Disemboweling a stoat with a soup spoon

3. Shouting to judges, *"Don't forget last night at the Marriott!"*

2. You don't give a rat's ass about world peace

1. Stop smiling for a couple of seconds

TOP TEN WAYS TO MISPRONOUNCE BIBI NETANYAHU

10. Yahoo Netanbibi

9. Bibi Nut & Honey

8. Bibi Netan Yo-Yo Ma

7. Hey Mindy Nanu Nanu

6. Bibi Hears a Who

5. "Weird Bibi" Netanyankovic

4. Scooby Doo Where Are You

3. Anfernee Hardaway

2. Bibi or Not Bibi

1. Baby I'm-a Want You

TOP TEN SIGNS THERE SHOULDN'T BE A SECOND DATE

10. Every time you start to speak, your date screams

9. She says, "Just a guess—but have you ever done any sideshow work?"

8. He has passionate opinions about which Olson twin is the most talented

7. She keeps making out with that other guy she brought along

6. He insists you watch how far he can spit soup

5. She excuses herself to use the rest room at a different restaurant

4. He's made up like Joan Crawford

3. You notice more than one granddaddy longlegs on his suit

2. At the end of the evening, she bashfully asks if she could have one of your ears

1. He says, "You kiss even better than Mom!"

TOP TEN LEAST POPULAR BROADWAY SHOWS

10. *Les Cheez Whizerables*

9. *I'll Paint Any Wagon for Just $99.99*

8. *Sunday in the Park with George "Goober" Lindsey*

7. *Okay, Okay—I Am Rappaport*

6. *Kiss Me Kate and I'll Sue You for Sexual Harassment*

5. *Don King and I*

4. *The Really Really Odd Couple Starring Tony Randall and a Giant Squid*

3. *Damn Yankees, Fuckin' Mets*

2. *Shelley Winters Wordlessly Consumes an Entire Pot Roast to the Music of Cole Porter*

1. *The Best Little Whorehouse in Newark*

TOP TEN SIGNS BORIS YELTSIN IS IN GOOD HEALTH

10. Easily runs down two flights of stairs when he hears the bells of the ice cream truck

9. While still red, his nose no longer emits that sizzling sound

8. Just filmed a new infomercial for his "Yeltsinizer" exercise machine

7. Was seen scaling Kremlin walls in his Spiderman suit

6. Ear-piercing wolf whistles at fat ladies in babushkas

5. Once again wrestling his pet bear for the table scraps

4. Opened last night as the new Norma Desmond in *Sunset Boulevard*

3. His ass no longer looks like a breakaway republic

2. Blood alcohol level back up to a healthy 53 percent

1. Looks almost as good as the preserved body of Lenin

TOP TEN NEW McDONALD'S OFFERINGS FOR ADULTS

10. Quarter Fucking Pounder with Goddamn Cheese

9. Nicotine Nuggets

8. McMetamucil Shake

7. The Two-Hookers-and-Charlie-Sheen Sandwich

6. Super Size 32-ounce Martini

5. Double Order of Fries Served in One of Pamela Anderson's Old Bras

4. Ronald Wallbanger

3. Lapdance from the Assistant Manager

2. Actual Meat

1. Happy Meal with Prozac

TOP TEN LEAST POPULAR VALENTINE'S CARDS

10. "Thinking of You, Sweetheart . . . Which, Technically, the Court Order Can't Prevent"

9. "Just Wanted to Say 'I Love You' When I Wasn't Falling-Down Drunk"

8. "If Only We Weren't So Closely Related"

7. "Even Though I'm a Bosnian Serb, You're My Favorite Croat Muslim!"

6. "I'm Too Shy to Ask in Person, but What's That Thing on Your Face? A Wart? A Mole? *What?*"

5. "You're Too Beautiful to Resist, My Under-the-Ether Dental Patient"

4. "I'm More Than Half-Interested in You, My Hermaphrodite Darling"

3. "The Medicated Shampoo Took Care of It"

2. "I'm Glad the Arkansas State Troopers Brought You Up to My Hotel Room, Valentine"

1. "I'll Give You Money to Have Sex with Me"

TOP TEN WAYS TO DISCOURAGE TEENS FROM SMOKING

10. Start rumor that cigarettes cause acne

9. Explain that it spoils the taste of crack

8. Ask, "Don't you want to be around for *Dick Clark's Rockin' New Year's Eve 2050 A.D.*?"

7. Show them hidden camera footage of Joe Camel hacking up big black wads of gunk

6. Point out how chances of having illicit sex improve if you don't smell like an ashtray

5. Every time you see them smoking, have that old Indian actor go over to them with a single tear running down his cheek

4. Remove cigarette machines from New York City schoolrooms

3. Tell them they *have* to smoke! If I know teenagers, that's exactly what they *won't* do! Am I right?

2. Lavish ad campaign featuring "The Marlboro Geek"

1. Four words: Photo of Keith Richards

TOP TEN REJECTED COLLEGE FOOTBALL CHEERS

10. You don't have to stay ahead!
    You just have to beat the spread!

9. Pass it high! Pass it low!
   Pass it like Dad's kidney stone!

8. We want some touchdowns!
   Not a bunch of Hugh Downs!

7. Our school recruits illiterate athletes!
   YAYYYYYYY!

6. If you're a hermaphrodite and you know it,
   Why don't you stand up and show it?

5. *Gimmee an E!*
   Gimmee an H!
   Gimmee an H!
   Gimmee an H!
   Gimmee an H!
   What's that spell?
   Ehhhh.

4. Apple, cherry, lemon, orange!
   Uh-oh, nothing rhymes with orange!

3. YEEEAAHHH! They've got guns!

2. Attention, owner of a Chevy Lumina,
   license 1EJ78, your lights are on

1. What does it matter who wins the game?
   In a hundred years we'll be dead just the
   same!

TOP TEN PROBLEMS AT HOOTERS

10. Losing money on "D-cup of coffee"

9. Environmentalists complaining about the Spotted Owl fritters

8. Loose, shapeless uniforms keep shrinking in the dryer

7. The FDA found silicone implants in the chicken breasts

6. Tanked-up Martha Stewart always getting in shoving matches over at the Mortal Kombat game

5. Workers' compensation claims way up for halter rash

4. Waitresses too often return to the university professorships from which they've taken sabbaticals

3. Some of the brighter customers have figured out they can make mediocre hamburgers at home

2. Ted Kennedy's unpaid bar tab now in the six figures

1. Competition from International House of Bimbos

TOP TEN SHOCKING REVELATIONS IN THE WHITEWATER HEARINGS

10. The Clintons got the funds from Mr. Drysdale's bank with the help of Miss Hathaway

9. Democrats blaming death of Vince Foster on his sons, Lyle and Erik Foster

8. Al D'Amato admitting he's only holding the hearings to impress Amy Fisher

7. "Whitewater" named in honor of Barry White

6. Bill once made a sandwich out of two doughnuts and a Gainesburger

5. Crucial missing documents had been used by Chelsea to make a papier-mâché volcano for school

4. During intense questioning, President Clinton's sudden claim that he doesn't speak English

3. Bruce Wayne and Batman *are the same guy*

2. Whitewater now site of Retirement Home for Gubernatorial Mistresses

1. Nobody gives a rat's ass about the whole thing

TOP TEN LEAST POPULAR BREAKFAST CEREALS

10. Trichinosis Pops

9. Vlasic Dill Krispies

8. Deafeningly Loud Cracklin' Oat Bran

7. Fruit & Fibre 'n Fire Ants

6. Ordinary K

5. Nature Valley 100 Percent Sodium Benzoate Flakes

4. Seagram's Liquor Puffs

3. Pissed-Off Black Panther Cream of Wheat

2. Well, *Almost* All-Bran

1. Calvin Klein's Obsession for Breakfast

TOP TEN THINGS ON THE POPE'S "TO DO" LIST

10. Canonize everyone connected with Pringles, the stackable potato chip

9. Perform exorcism on Richard Simmons

8. Memorize some really snappy Presbyterian jokes

7. Pitch idea for cameo as Murphy Brown's secretary

6. Think of diplomatic way to advise Clinton to "Cool it with the broads, Bubba"

5. Contact Ovitz for conference call with God

4. Get Popemobile rigged so it hops up and down like Dr. Dre's Impala

3. Forgive Letterman for hosting Academy Awards

2. New papal edict: "Be Your Own Dog: Drink Red Dog Beer!"

1. Respond to some obvious question with "Hey, am I Catholic?"

TOP TEN SIGNS THE OTHER BEATLES DON'T LIKE YOU

10. Whenever you start talking, they say, "Let it be, bonehead"

9. When the band appeared on *Sullivan,* you had to share a dressing room with a seal

8. You find out you were the inspiration for "Nowhere Man"

7. After you spent weeks working on a painting for the cover, they decide to go with "The White Album"

6. You come into the studio and find your sitar smashed into a thousand pieces

5. Keep assigning you to tour with *Beatlemania*

4. Repeatedly cracking you on the skull with silver hammers

3. You're still waiting to find out whether any of those records you all put out ever made any money

2. Always trying to set you up with Yoko

1. They tell you, "We hear the Stones are hiring"

TOP TEN THINGS OVERHEARD AT THE WHITE HOUSE THANKSGIVING DINNER

10. "Commander in Chief to Air Force One: Release gravy bomb."

9. "Do they always make Warren Christopher eat at the kids' table?"

8. "Mmmmm, deep-fried cranberries."

7. "Thank you, Lord, for making the Republicans so old and unlikable that everybody's forgotten what a load I am."

6. "This turkey died after Newt Gingrich cut off its Medicaid funding."

5. "Sorry about Socks, sir, but the Laser-Guided Carving System *is* just a Pentagon prototype. . . ."

4. "The president has definitely decided on light meat—no, wait . . . make that dark meat—no, now he's saying light meat—no, he's changed it to dark again—"

3. "It's officially Thanksgiving—Roger just passed out in his mashed potatoes."

2. "Mr. Perot has brought a couple of pie charts showing what kind of pie we have this year."

1. "Let's go to the living room and watch high-altitude satellite pictures of football."

TOP TEN LEAST POPULAR BREEDS OF DOG

10. Hairless Borgnine

9. Twenty-Legged Dachshund

8. Doberman Fainter

7. Irish Boozehound

6. Two-Assed Setter

5. Pug with the Head of Leon Panetta

4. Mexican Tick Wagon

3. Holocaust-Denying German Shepherd

2. Flying Incontinent Chihuahua

1. Self-Neutering Corgi

TOP TEN FIDEL CASTRO PICKUP LINES

10. "I have no hard currency, but if I did, could I buy you a drink?"

9. "When I look at you, I get a 'Cuban missile crisis'!"

8. "Would you mind checking my beard for ticks?"

7. "Want to come back to my crumbling palace for a ten-year-old tin of Soviet sardines?"

6. "You're even prettier than Khrushchev."

5. "Can I store my cigar in your humidor?"

4. "These day-long breadlines are full of phonies. Let's go someplace quiet."

3. "You may never get another chance to do it with a commie."

2. "I could hide out in your hills indefinitely!"

1. "I can't spell Cuba without *U*!"

TOP TEN THINGS THAT WILL GET YOU KICKED OFF A JURY

10. Whenever prosecutor approaches the jury box, attempt to give him your drink order

9. Snoring so loudly it wakes the other jurors

8. Asking for a conjugal visit with the judge's wife

7. When items are held up to be entered as evidence, shout out a bid

6. Snickering loudly whenever a witness swears to tell the truth

5. Wearing one of them rainbow wigs and carrying a JOHN 3:12 sign

4. Every chance you get, leap from your seat and wrestle the service revolver away from a court officer

3. Show up for three consecutive days with pie on your face

2. Every time somebody objects, knock back a Jell-O shot

1. Refusing to remove your Walkman

MARTHA STEWART'S TOP TEN WORST TIPS FOR LIVING

10. If you notice a guest using the wrong fork at dinner, pick up the right fork and jam it into his head

9. Nothing spruces up a bathroom like potpourri and a big stack of wrestling magazines

8. Spray-paint a couple of pomegranates gold and hurl them through the windshield of a police car

7. Heavily sedated pets make unusual centerpieces

6. Keep tall piles of old newspapers all around the house for that "crazy old hermit" look

5. Save time and money with a Reynolds Wrap coffin

4. After those pod people from outer space hatch, their empty pods make terrific catchalls

3. To show your host you enjoyed your meal, let loose with a foghorn belch

2. When applying wood stain, make sure there's no ventilation so you'll get totally wasted

1. Add glitter to every damn thing you own

TOP TEN MOVIES PLAYING IN TIMES SQUARE

10. *The Slutty Professor*

9. *Pantsless in Seattle*

8. *Jane and Her Giant Peaches*

7. *The Loin King*

6. *Breakfast on Tiffany*

5. *Hannah and Her Sisters and the Pizza Delivery Boy*

4. *Three Men and a Gerbil*

3. *Pretty "Woman"*

2. *Sir Edmund Climbs Hillary*

1. *Howard's End*

TOP TEN SURPRISING FACTS ABOUT DR. KEVORKIAN

10. Has a sign over his house that says OVER 25 PEOPLE KILLED

9. Doesn't charge for his work; earns money as a male stripper

8. Sometimes replaces the poison he ordinarily uses in lethal injections with Folgers Crystals

7. On weekends, Suicide Machine doubles as Lotto Ping-Pong Ball Selector

6. At dinner, loves to play joke where he screams, *"Oh my God! Did you drink that?!"*

5. Secretly thinks the nickname "Dr. Death" is really cool

4. Once overheard guy on bus say, "I'd rather die than go to work today" and strangled him on the spot with his own belt

3. Once got sued for malpractice by a patient he accidentally healed

2. Only reason he got plum "Suicide Doctor" job is because his daddy is Aaron Spelling

1. Never killed a man he didn't like

TOP TEN REJECTED STORIES ON *ENTERTAINMENT TONIGHT*

10. Hollywood's Top Stars Turn Out to Loot a Derailed Freight Train

9. Why the Pillsbury Doughboy and Snuggle the Fabric Softener Bear Hate Each Other's Guts

8. Sandy Duncan: Mafia Kingpin

7. Artist Formerly Known As Prince Changes Dog's Name to "The Dog Formerly Known As Prince's Dog"

6. Scandal at that Sally Struthers Correspondence School: She Only Teaches *Some* of the Courses!

5. Whatever Happened to Patty Duke's Twin Sister?

4. The Bitter Rivalry Between Larry King's Left Suspender and Larry King's Right Suspender

3. Nude Photos of Madonna Found

2. What to Do If Ozzy Osbourne Bites You

1. More Trouble with Hell's Angels at John Tesh Concerts

TOP TEN REASONS YASSER ARAFAT WILL MAKE A GOOD FATHER

10. Colicky infants soothed by the feel of stubble

9. Plastic explosives pick up comic-strip ink better than Silly Putty

8. Can force UN to recognize kid as "Cutest Baby on the West Bank"

7. For show-and-tell, daddy can help the kid build a bitchin' car bomb

6. Skyjackings mean cheap, fun family vacation trips

5. Take an old sock, stuff it with beard clippings, and presto—a teething toy

4. Already knows the words to all the Barney songs

3. If this Palestinian presidential thing doesn't work out, he can always support his family driving a New York City cab

2. Sure winner at Parents' Day Ringo Look-Alike Contest

1. Peekaboo with the headdress

TOP TEN REJECTED *STAR TREK* CHARACTERS

10. "Bones" Epstein, the Ship's Dermatologist

9. The Pillsbury Dough Android

8. Rhoda, the Neurotic Upstairs Neighbor

7. Flatulor

6. Skip, the Space Intern from Cornell

5. 975-Year-Old Bob Hope

4. Frank, the Half Human–Half Italian

3. Shatner's Recklessly Reproducing Hairpiece

2. Gary, the Friendless Geek Who Reads a Lot of Sci-Fi and Hasn't Had Sex in Light-Years

1. Jimmy the Astro-Hamster

TOP TEN OTHER O.J. DEFENSE RHYMES

10. DNA? Give me a break—
    It's too small to see, for heaven's sake!

9. The Bronco's idling right outside,
   So acquit the man and let him ride

8. Even if you think he did all this stuff,
   Wasn't playing for the Bills punishment
   enough?

7. If the mood is right and I feel a spark,
   I wouldn't mind nailing Marcia Clark

6. If you think about Fuhrman, it'll
   Make you vote for an acquitt'l

5. Make the right decision, one and all,
   And you'll each take home an autographed
   football

4. Here's our case:
   It was guys from outer space

3. If it really *does* fit,
   Then we're in deep shit

2. Our poetry sucks—
   But we've made six million bucks

1. Evidence, shmevidence

TOP TEN SIGNS YOU'VE HIRED THE WRONG KID TO MOW YOUR LAWN

10. He shows up with a pair of nail clippers and a Ziploc bag

9. On the side of his mower you notice the stenciled silhouettes of thirteen cats

8. Stops frequently to nap inside the grass-catcher

7. Always trying to impress you by stopping the mower blades with his head

6. You notice him shoving the last of his clothes into the mulcher

5. He's fascinated by the details of your home security system

4. Stops every couple of minutes to smoke some clippings

3. Somehow manages to mow the hood ornament off your Lexus

2. Turns a goat loose and says he'll be back in three weeks

1. No toes

TOP TEN LEAST POPULAR BEVERAGES

10. Kraft Root Beer & Cheese

9. Lyme Disease Rickey

8. Broccoli Daiquiri

7. Sherwin-Williams Exterior Latex on the Rocks

6. *E. coli* Colada

5. Sunblock 'n Seltzer

4. Fanta Air Conditioner Drippings

3. Stamp Glue Spritzer

2. Watermelon Juice Squeezed Out of Gallagher's Beard

1. Crapple

TOP TEN THINGS LISA MARIE MISSES ABOUT BEING MARRIED TO MICHAEL JACKSON

10. Cosmetics companies always sending cartons of free samples

9. Hyperbaric chamber a great place to keep baked goods fresh

8. Instant line of credit with every plastic surgeon west of the Rockies

7. The cute way he'd get angry when salesmen would ask him to put Mommy on the phone

6. Sneak previews of Liz Taylor's latest hip X rays

5. The adorable sheepish way he'd tell her that he had to pay off another kid

4. On picnics, his old noses made great corn-on-the-cob holders

3. The monkey smell

2. The way his billions of dollars looked so nice next to her billions of dollars

1. That special surge of desire a woman feels for her man when she sees him clutching a stuffed bunny on a merry-go-round

TOP TEN SURPRISING NEW BEST-SELLERS

10. *Delicate Eye Surgery for Dummies*

9. *Bob Vila's How to Torch It for the Insurance Money*

8. *Kama Sutra for One*

7. *Julia Child's Recipes Involving Lots and Lots of Cooking Sherry*

6. *The Prison Haiku of Mike Tyson*

5. *All Things Flea-and-Tick-Infested* by James Herriot

4. *Chicks Dig Physics* by Stephen Hawking

3. *The Pair of Glasses That Took Almost Two Hours to Make: A Horror Story from LensCrafters*

2. *Martha Stewart's Guide to Oral Sex at Drive-Ins*

1. *If Al Franken Were a 25-Pound Turkey I'd Fill Him with Plenty of Delicious Stuffing and Roast Him to a Golden Brown and Then Eat Every Bit of Him Right Down to the Bones* by Rush Limbaugh

TOP TEN ANNA NICOLE SMITH DATING TIPS

10. Forget personal ads—try the intensive-care unit

9. Wear something that, even to his failing eyes, will look slutty

8. Make sure the valet parkers understand: If he dies in the restaurant, you get the car

7. Remind him, "Hey, when you're 160, I'll be 101!"

6. To convincingly fake excitement during lovemaking, just think about his stock portfolio

5. Good pickup line: "Can I pre-chew that for you?"

4. For fifty bucks, Tiffany will engrave a hearing aid

3. Learn as much as you can about the two *P*'s: Prostate and Probate

2. When he wants sex, hide his glasses and put him in bed with a car battery

1. Low-cut dress + small amount of blood to brain = marriage proposal

TOP TEN LEAST POPULAR NATIONAL PUBLIC RADIO SHOWS

10. *Garrison Keillor's Big & Tall Men's Loose Suit Giveaway*

9. *Spotted Owl Recipe Roundup*

8. *NEA Secretary Jane Alexander Counts Down the Hits*

7. *30 Minutes of Tax Dollars Crackling in a Bonfire*

6. *Folk Songs About Ear, Nose & Throat Problems*

5. *The Right-Wing Militia Compound Home Companion*

4. *Rap Music Today with George Plimpton*

3. *The "Car Talk" Guys Add Up Long Columns of Two-Digit Numbers in a Boston Accent*

2. *Newt Gingrich Presents an Hour of Dead Air*

1. *All Things Considered Sticky*

TOP TEN SIGNS YOUR PICNIC SUCKS

10. The "caraway seeds" in the coleslaw look suspiciously like deer ticks

9. That Red Dog from the beer commercials gets drunk and tries to mate with your roast chicken

8. Your original campfire has now consumed 10,000 acres

7. After two quarts of Colt .45, Roseanne starts showing everybody her tattoos

6. Crazy mix-up leaves you with a cooler containing some guy's liver transplant

5. Three-legged race won by wife's three-legged uncle

4. An angry Yasser Arafat appears from woods to snatch your tablecloth and put it back on his head

3. You're a soccer player from Colombia and your plane just crashed

2. Your picnic companion is inflatable

1. O.J. keeps "accidentally" hitting people with lawn darts

TOP TEN PERKS OF WINNING AN ACADEMY AWARD

10. Sensual massage from both Price and Waterhouse

9. Free "Ask Me About My Oscar" bumper sticker

8. Right to spit on Pauly Shore with impunity

7. Unlimited use of the Academy Award Winners Lounge at any Dunkin' Donuts

6. Statuette can be wedged in steering wheel to deter car thieves

5. For the rest of your life, any "leaner" you get in horseshoes automatically counts as a "ringer"

4. Right of first refusal for lead role in any and all upcoming *Police Academy* movies

3. Access to thousands of hilarious, never-before-seen Dom DeLuise/Burt Reynolds bloopers

2. 50 percent off Heidi Fleiss

1. Get a big tax deduction donating all the cheap crap in your closet to Planet Hollywood

TOP TEN SURPRISING FACTS ABOUT NEWT GINGRICH

10. A conservative in Washington, he's an ultraliberal in the cracker-and-cookie aisle

9. His mom now has Connie Chung doing yard work

8. Uses Speaker's gavel to tenderize meat

7. Will make love to his wife only after she says, "I yield to the Congressman from Georgia"

6. Gets 13 albums for a penny, then quits and joins again

5. Hair turned white after a really scary episode of *Tales from the Crypt*

4. Once paid a hooker $1,000 to read the Contract with America all the way through

3. For all his anti-PBS talk, wears Bert & Ernie slippers around the house

2. Has launched his own probe into Hillary, if you know what I mean

1. Sometimes, very late at night, he actually shuts the hell up

TOP TEN DEMANDS OF THE FREEMEN IN MONTANA

10. A year's supply of Turtle Wax

9. President Clinton and other top officials must attend their karaoke night and applaud politely

8. An ATF agent to reset their VCR clock for Daylight Savings Time

7. Replace the "Toys for Guns" program with a "Guns for Toys" program

6. A scale model of their compound made entirely from Nilla wafers

5. Guarantee that Susan Lucci will finally win a daytime Emmy award

4. It sounds incredible, but they want Kraft Macaroni & Cheese to taste *even cheesier*

3. A better publicist

2. When they go to trial, they want that O.J. jury

1. A busload of "freewomen"

TOP TEN WAYS THE COUNTRY WOULD BE DIFFERENT IF IT WERE RUN BY MODELS

10. Lots of public-service announcements on how to make yourself throw up

9. American flag redesigned with vertical stripes for a more "slimming" effect

8. President vetoes legislation by making a pouty look

7. Oath of Office would include phrase "I solemnly swear to have fabulously long coltlike legs"

6. Head of FBI: Mr. Blackwell

5. Face of guy who invented no-smudge mascara added to Mt. Rushmore

4. Constitution repealed in favor of document reading "Like, *whatever*"

3. Supreme Court justices wear robes from Victoria's Secret

2. Punishment for all crimes: Eat a huge cake

1. New cabinet-level official: Buttmaster General

TOP TEN NEW PHARMACEUTICALS BANNED BY THE FDA

10. Solar-Powered Pacemaker

9. Vasectomy-in-a-Can

8. U-Fit-'Em Glass Eyes Grab Bag

7. Johnson & Johnson Possibly Sterile Bargain Band-Aids

6. Edible Cast from Pillsbury

5. Elmer's Esophagus Glue

4. Dr. Scholl's Raw Veal Insoles

3. Scotch Brand Adhesive Skin Grafts

2. Ouija Board Blood Pressure Guesser

1. Oscar Mayer All-Beef Marital Aid

TOP TEN THINGS OVERHEARD ON THE MILLION-MAN MARCH

10. "Gag spinning bow ties! Get your gag spinning bow ties here!"

9. "I think Farrakhan puts on a much better show since he added the Farrakhanettes."

8. "Listen! You can hear President Clinton flip-flopping from here!"

7. "I'm sorry, but I think your disguise is in very poor taste, Mr. Danson."

6. "Farrakhan? Damn, I was waiting to see *Chaka Khan!*"

5. "I'd like to thank Pee-Wee Herman for lending me the suit."

4. "All this *schlepping* is making me *meshugenah!*"

3. "I can't wait to see the expression on their faces when we walk into Denny's and say, 'Farrakhan, party of one million.' "

2. "Thank you, Mayor Barry, for keeping drugs off the street."

1. "One, two, three . . . ah, screw it—*a million!*"

TOP TEN SECRETS OF THE ROYAL FAMILY

10. Routinely pull rank to throw midnight keggers at Stonehenge

9. Queen Elizabeth has killed hundreds of her subjects by insisting on driving on the right side of the road

8. Diana used to dry her nylons by hanging them on Charles's ears

7. Original source of family's wealth: Chain of Windsor's Cut-Rate Lube Centers

6. Queen Mother had a passionate five-year affair with Benny Hill

5. Before the operation, Fergie went by the name "Nigel"

4. Latin motto on coat of arms roughly translates to "Inbred Dullards in Fancy Clothes"

3. Di once pawned the Crown Jewels to buy hair bleach

2. They were soundly beaten by the Jackson 5 in a seldom-aired 1971 taping of *Family Feud*

1. At home by themselves, none of them uses utensils

TOP TEN SIGNS YOU'RE AT A BAD SUMMER CAMP

10. The water level of the lake rises whenever someone flushes the toilet

9. It's located on a patch of I-95 median strip

8. Each cabin is named after a different member of the Van Patten family

7. "Arts & Crafts" involves long hours in a sweaty cabin sewing budget sportswear for Kmart

6. Have to toast marshmallows by laying them on exhaust pipe of counselor's Chevy

5. The camp offers a trophy for "Excellence in Making Fun of the Kid with Asthma"

4. Campfire stories consist of counselor recalling the time he "knifed a screw in the joint"

3. Every night a mysterious truck pulls up and takes a half-dozen kids to a place called the Neverland Ranch

2. Nightly sing-alongs to that "Isn't It Ironic?" song

1. You end up having an 81-day standoff with the FBI

TOP TEN WAYS TO MAKE HOCKEY MORE EXCITING

10. Goalie removes an article of clothing for each point allowed

9. If the Zamboni goes less than 50 mph, it blows up

8. Canadians must play in bare feet

7. Replace hockey sticks with live flamingos

6. Just barely visible under the ice: The frozen body of Walt Disney

5. At some point in every game—exciting police chase in the stands

4. Actually have Jason from *Friday the 13th* skating around in his hockey mask trying to kill guys

3. Instead of an ice rink, a huge red-hot griddle covered in bacon grease

2. One word: Blindfolds

1. Lose the puck and goals—and just make it a four-period free-for-all

TOP TEN LEAST POPULAR T-SHIRT SLOGANS

10. "Ask Me About My 23 Other Distinct Personalities"

9. "Steve Lawrence Is God"

8. "Honorary Menendez Brother"

7. "This Shirt Shoplifted in New York City"

6. "Not a Grateful Dead Fan—Just Naturally Fucked Up"

5. " 'Where's the Beef?' 10th Anniversary Commemorative from the Franklin Mint"

4. "I Survived a Brief Marriage to Shannen Doherty"

3. "Legalize Headcheese"

2. "Hey, Super-Logical Robot! This Is *Not* a T-Shirt! Whaddya Make of That? Huh?"

1. "Camp Ebert"

TOP TEN SIGNS YOU'RE IN AN UNSAFE AIRPORT

10. Parking lot has sign: NOT RESPONSIBLE FOR CARS DAMAGED BY FALLING AIRCRAFT

9. Machines sell insurance just for your time in the airport

8. You see a limo driver holding up a sign: AVOWED TERRORIST

7. Mary Jo Buttafuoco walks through metal detector without her bullet setting it off

6. The ground crew is bringing the jet fuel to the plane in their cupped hands

5. At check-in, agent reminds you you're limited to two carry-on explosives

4. Runways have passing lanes

3. As you board plane, gate attendant says, "You poor son of a bitch"

2. Cheering crowd has gathered in lounge around a pilot doing ten shots of Stoli in a row

1. Hijackers are allowed to preboard

TOP TEN THINGS A BALLERINA WOULD NEVER SAY

10. "It's like a dream come true! Tomorrow at this time, I'll actually be *Mrs.* Boxcar Willie!"

9. "When I have to jump really high, I pretend there's a rottweiler biting me in the ass."

8. "Whoa, Molly! That second rack of ribs ain't sitting right!"

7. "I can't get the chewing-tobacco stains out of my unitard."

6. "Baseball players can scratch themselves—why can't I?"

5. "Don't get me started about my favorite Stooge!"

4. "You move that piece-of-crap truck of yours, cowboy, or I'll force-feed you your own lungs."

3. "Wanna hear me belch the national anthem?"

2. "Hey, girls! Let's go beat the crap outta some opera singers!"

1. "Better back off—I think I'm gonna hurl from all this spinnin'!"

TOP TEN ITEMS REMAINDERED BY KMART

10. Wham-O Brand Lingerie

9. Hillshire Farms Monkey Sausage Sampler

8. Rollerblade Snow Chains

7. Jeff Foxworthy Video: *You Might Have Driven This Whole Redneck Thing into the Ground If . . .*

6. Right-on-Your-Arm Chigger Farm

5. Michael Jackson's Old Noses Nesting Dolls

4. Virtual Reality Gloves & Goggle Set Simulating the Line at the DMV

3. Home Liposuction Attachment for Vacuum Cleaner

2. Olaf, the Live-In Swede with the Personality Disorder

1. CNN's *Crossfire:* The Home Game

TOP TEN WAYS TO FORFEIT A BASEBALL GAME

10. Players' blood alcohol level higher than their on-base percentage

9. When you get ball, don't throw it. Swallow it.

8. Repeatedly calling the umpire "madame"

7. Your first baseman? Ty Cobb's corpse

6. Persistent pattern of fielders taking bites from fans' hot dogs when leaning into stands to catch fly balls

5. Have stadium announcer start "outing" players

4. Guy bringing on new pitcher in bullpen cart intentionally runs over opposing team's base runner

3. Fans fail to complete the Wave

2. Being caught wearing the still-experimental Wonder Cup

1. Catcher fails to pass local emission standards

TOP TEN GOLFER PET PEEVES

10. You decide to call your restaurant "The 19th Hole" and damn it if somebody hasn't thought of it already!

9. Chicks who are just using you to meet Dorf

8. When another golfer drinks too much beer and becomes a water hazard

7. People who see you in your golf outfit and just assume you're gay

6. Beatniks who use the 15th fairway for one of their "happenings"

5. During sex with your wife, she murmurs "slice"

4. When an X ray reveals you've got two dozen tees in your stomach

3. Having to go to the hospital after trying a little "experiment" with the ball washer

2. When your zoeller gets all fuzzy

1. Caddies with Tourette's syndrome

TOP TEN GOOD THINGS ABOUT RAISING THE SPEED LIMIT

10. Lovely fall foliage tours with Al Unser, Jr.

9. Better head start to smash through police barricades

8. Sound of wind passing through grille is just like having a free Yoko Ono CD!

7. Lots of laughs when you make a hitchhiker's pants blow off

6. Yankee players have better chance of making it home before drugs kick in

5. Fun to shout, *"Hello-Rhode-Island-good-bye-Rhode-Island!"*

4. Have to hear much less of Kathie Lee on Thanksgiving as Macy's parade now only takes ten minutes

3. Cool to glance over at car next to you and get a big thumbs-up from James Brown

2. Joy of making passenger Ralph Nader wet his pants

1. Now much more difficult for Smokey to stop the Bandit

TOP TEN WAYS TO MAKE ELECTIONS MORE EXCITING

10. Make outcome completely unpredictable by having ballots counted by New York high school students

9. Call it "Vote-a-palooza"

8. Candidate says secret word—gets hit with bag of flour

7. Fill the voting booths with rotting meat; then just sit back and wait for the hyenas!

6. Every field of candidates must contain at least one nutty billionaire

5. More frequent use of the word *hustings*

4. Fly in Dukakis, put him in a tank, and laugh till your nuts fall off!

3. In final week of campaign, every speech has to rhyme

2. Loser gets lethal injection . . . Oh, what the hell, *winner gets lethal injection, too!*

1. You don't pull the voting booth's lever—it pulls yours

TOP TEN REASONS LOIS LANE IS DUMPING SUPERMAN

10. She's now totally deaf in one ear because of his super snoring

9. Every time he left toilet seat up, blamed it on Clark Kent

8. Always making wisecracks about how his X-ray vision couldn't penetrate her meat loaf

7. Has no problem stopping a powerful locomotive, but try asking him to mow the lawn

6. His insistence that the kids be raised super

5. Won't ask directions even after he's been flying around lost for hours

4. He always had to go "stop a tidal wave" whenever her parents were in town

3. He may be evil, but at least Lex Luthor has a car

2. Saw him barhopping in the Village in a Wonder Woman outfit

1. Tired of excuses like "There must be some kryptonite under the bed"

TOP TEN SIGNS VLADIMIR ZHIRINOVSKY IS NUTS

10. Shows his hypernationalism by chugging a bottle of Russian dressing three times a day

9. Asked Marge Schott to be his date to the annual Bigots' Picnic

8. Nightly checkers games with the propped-up cadaver of Joe Stalin

7. Wants to replace KGB with the Psychic Friends Network

6. The "Hitler Is Groovy" tattoo

5. Claims he's the father of Pamela Anderson's baby

4. Uses scrambled military phone lines to order porcelain ballerinas from the Home Shopping Network

3. Locks himself in room for days at a time to play with a set of those little nesting dolls

2. Lost his virginity to a turnip

1. Now referring to himself as "The Clown Prince of Baseball"

TOP TEN TV SHOW WARNINGS

10. *Montel Williams:* "Reflections off Mr. Williams's head may induce seizures in epileptics."

9. *America's Funniest Home Videos:* "May contain some Canadian and/or Mexican home videos."

8. *Murder, She Wrote:* "The murder victim you are about to see is a trained professional. Do not try getting killed at home."

7. *The Fresh Prince of Bel Air:* "Prince no longer fresh after August 15."

6. *ER:* "Odds are 1 in 1 million your doctor will look anything like George Clooney."

5. *Mr. Rogers' Neighborhood:* "Caution: Them puppets is creepy."

4. *Baywatch:* "Acting quality impaired by seawater trapped in actors' inner ears."

3. *MTV News:* "Does not contain actual news."

2. *America's Most Wanted:* "If you happen to watch this broadcast with any of these dudes, they'll probably kill you."

1. *The Nanny:* "Sound of Fran Drescher's voice may cause impotence."

TOP TEN TENNIS-PRO PICKUP LINES

10. "Ever done it on clay?"

9. "I've got a mattress made out of John McEnroe's old sweatbands."

8. "Let's go back to my place and work on your grip."

7. "Have you ever heard of the 'Pants Open'?"

6. "Wanna hear me grunt like Monica Seles?"

5. "How about a little horizontal volley?"

4. "Have my child and I'll give it free tennis lessons."

3. "Suddenly, there's an out–of–bounds in my pants."

2. "Dennis, anyone?"
(PROS NAMED DENNIS ONLY)

1. "I'd like to bjorn your borg!"

TOP TEN SIGNS YOU'RE IN A BAD MALL

10. Most upscale business: Day-Old Bread Mart

9. When you ride the escalator, you hear muffled screams coming from beneath your feet

8. Cosmetics salesgirl sprays perfume directly in your eyes

7. It has two organ stores

6. There's a shop called Victor's Secret

5. "Food court" is two lawn chairs and an open box of Ritz crackers

4. Couple of guys floating facedown in the fountain

3. One store having a sale on lost children

2. There's an old bearded character inviting everybody to sit on his lap—but he ain't Santa

1. They've got a Gap for Losers

TOP TEN WAYS TO BEAT THE HEAT IN NEW YORK CITY

10. Stand on sidewalk; catch air conditioners as they fall out of apartment windows

9. Leave your car unattended just long enough to get the doors stolen

8. Go to Times Square and score a crack Slurpee

7. Lash together a couple of East River mob corpses and go rafting

6. Get shot by Bernie Goetz, sue for $43 million, and buy yourself a top-of-the-line fan

5. When counterman at Baskin-Robbins asks, "Cup or cone?," say, "In my shorts, scoop dude"

4. Ask cabbie to drive you to airport, then enjoy pleasant side trip through Maine

3. Apply for a job as one of New York's "Official Pantsless Psychotics"

2. Ask guy near Lincoln Tunnel entrance to squeegee your forehead

1. Carjack Mister Softee

TOP TEN SOLDIER PET PEEVES

10. Finding out the *C* in C rations stands for "cat"

9. Officers who won't accept the finger as a "New York salute"

8. You're on amphibious maneuvers and you just can't stop giggling

7. When your tank mates have been eating Mexican food

6. Marching with fixed bayonets and the guy behind you doesn't hear "halt!"

5. Mediocre in-flight magazine on troop transports

4. Getting hit with some "friendly fire" in the latrine

3. *"Alfa-Bravo-Foxtrot-Charlie"*—I mean, what the hell is *up* with that shit?

2. Camouflage fatigues make your ass look huge

1. Whenever you screw up, somebody starts singing that "Be All That You Can Be" song real sarcastically

TOP TEN SIGNS YOU'RE NOT GOING TO GRADUATE FROM HIGH SCHOOL THIS YEAR

10. During the fittings for caps and gowns, you're sent out to the football field to look for four-leaf clovers

9. Your only English paper was titled "*TV Guide:* Gateway to Viewing Pleasure"

8. You miss a lot of classes to appear in lineups

7. During final exams, teachers ask you to go out and get their lunch

6. Your rebuttal in the first round of the debate tournament: "You've convinced me!"

5. Nobody believes the pot in your locker was planted by "those Whitewater dudes"

4. Johnnie Cochran calls, asking you to serve on his next jury

3. They're giving you an incomplete in shop until you find the teacher's finger

2. It's nearly May and you still haven't found your homeroom

1. Your name: Kenny. This year's prom theme: *"Sorry You Won't Be Graduating, Kenny"*

TOP TEN CONSTRUCTION-WORKER PICKUP LINES

10. "Excuse me, would you mind brushing the sawdust out of my back hair?"

9. "Your skin looks as soft and pink as Owens-Corning fiberglass insulation."

8. "Union rules, miss—I have to inspect your foundation."

7. "You take my breath away, like that time I passed out in a septic tank."

6. "Haven't I yelled degrading comments at you somewhere before?"

5. "Ever seen a thumb contusion this bad?"

4. "I'm afraid of heights, miss—could you come up here and hold me?"

3. "I can introduce you to the other Village People."

2. "Yo"

1. "I'm 36 years old and still carry a box lunch. Doesn't that make you hot?"

TOP TEN SLOGANS FOR THE NEW FAT SUBSTITUTE OLESTRA

10. "Waddle over and buy some"

9. "Look like Siskel, eat like Ebert"

8. "Previously sold under the brand name Valvoline"

7. "Have you fit in a Ford lately?"

6. "Ten million fat guys can't be wrong"

5. "Tastes great with some Red Dye #4"

4. "Certified by the Mexican Food and Drug Administration"

3. "Get the picture, Poindexter? Like shit through a goose"

2. "We can't tell you exactly how we make it, but we can say this: Ten monkeys go into a room—and only nine come out"

1. "Word up, Tubby"

TOP TEN THINGS FOUND IN THE UNABOMBER'S CABIN

10. A fridge full of Swanson's "Hungry Psycho" frozen dinners

9. A gross of detonator caps from the Price Club

8. Half-full bottle of "Gee Your Scraggly Beard Smells Terrific" shampoo

7. Top hat, cane, and formal hooded sweatshirt

6. Tacked-up recipe for "tree-bark-and-spit casserole"

5. Rambling manifesto to *Penthouse* about the time two flight attendants needed help with a flat tire

4. Johnnie Cochran's business card

3. A crude "girlfriend" fashioned from an old mop, mud, and pinecones

2. Wacky sign on door: IF THIS CABIN'S TICKIN', BETTER RUN LIKE THE DICKENS!

1. Fifi, the "Unapoodle"

MARK FUHRMAN'S TOP TEN LAW-ENFORCEMENT TIPS

10. If you run out of blood to plant at a crime scene, try some jelly-doughnut filling

9. Win trust of African American community by declaring, "That Linc from *Mod Squad* is one happenin' dude!"

8. Plant one bloody glove: good
Plant two bloody gloves: better
Plant three bloody gloves: you're overdoing it, Jocko

7. When you're in doubt about anything, just ask yourself, "What would Adolf do?"

6. After a morning of beating up black guys, beat up a Mexican to "cleanse the palate"

5. A little Tabasco sauce on a lost kid's ice cream cone, and he'll start confessing to some major felonies

4. Insist you were talking about "chiggers"

3. Every Christmas, send a nice fruit basket to the boys in Internal Affairs

2. Keep your sorry ass a billion light-years away from Mike Tyson

1. Bill of Rights? More like *Load of Crap*!

TOP TEN THINGS THAT WILL GET YOU KICKED OUT OF THE KENTUCKY DERBY

10. Saddling and riding a member of the British royal family

9. Your horse's hoofprints are found on Whitewater documents

8. Stopping to pick up hitchhikers

7. DNA tests prove your "rare French Thoroughbred" is actually a dune buggy

6. Your name is Doug and you're selling "Doug Juleps"

5. You enter a monkey in a cowboy hat riding a collie

4. Flubber horseshoes

3. Abortive attempt to lead crowd in sing-along of "Horse with No Name"

2. Timothy Leary–style sugar cube treats

1. When your horse wins, he spikes the jockey

TOP TEN REJECTED NAMES FOR ROSS PEROT'S POLITICAL PARTY

10. The Rosstafarians

9. The Dork-o-crats

8. The Ice Cube in Hell Party

7. The You-Might-Be-a-Redneck-If-You-Join-This Party

6. The Wee-publicans

5. The Independents—Who Are Independent of Their Brains!

4. The Bloods

3. The RC Cola of Political Parties

2. The Adorable Miniature Candidate and His Friends

1. The Nutty Buddies

TOP TEN THINGS OVERHEARD AT AN NBA GAME

10. "It's time to start—Dennis Rodman's hair just turned green."

9. "Technical foul for putting a white guy in so early."

8. "That's odd. Soon Yi is yelling at Reggie Miller and Spike Lee is holding hands with Woody Allen."

7. "Will the squeegee guy please report to Charles Barkley's head?"

6. "Ladies and gentlemen, that last groin pull was brought to you by Nike!"

5. "Damn! Michael Jordan just quit to try professional hockey!"

4. "Isn't that adorable? Bob Costas just curled up and fell asleep in one of Scottie Pippen's shoes!"

3. "Mutombo, Shaquille. Shaquille, Mutombo. Mutombo and Shaquille—Kareem."

2. "According to Marv Albert's wife, he always beats the 24-second clock."

1. *"It's a new NBA record! $10 for a cup of beer!"*

TOP TEN SIGNS YOUR TV SHOW IS GOING TO BE CANCELED

10. The editors of *TV Guide* are currently working on a new super advanced version of the "jeer" just for your show

9. You've been preempted 138 weeks in a row

8. The chief surgeon in your tense medical drama is played by Carrot Top

7. While show is being broadcast, network runs a message along the bottom of the screen: *"Sorry about this crap"*

6. The number of your Amish viewers equals the number of your non-Amish viewers

5. It's a much-delayed attempt to cash in on the lambada craze

4. Research indicates that 99 percent of the people who fire guns at their TV happen to be watching your show at the time

3. You recently had to start sharing your studio with a Mexican game show

2. Entire cast is killed and their homes bulldozed in an end-of-season "cliffhanger"

1. According to Las Vegas oddsmakers, your show has less chance of coming back than Dean Martin

TOP TEN MISTAKES BILL CLINTON ADMITS HE'S MADE IN OFFICE

10. Too much flip-flopping; not enough shilly-shallying

9. After moving to White House, giving Roger the new address

8. Ordering Army Corps of Engineers to fill Potomac with gravy

7. Declaring a national holiday the day *Showgirls* was released

6. Not putting out the glue traps when Ross Perot dropped by

5. Would've liked to spend more time with beloved daughter What's-her-name

4. For first three years in office, thought it was *Bosco*-Herzegovina

3. Should've killed Newt Gingrich when he had the chance

2. Not getting Socks fixed

1. Not getting self fixed

TOP TEN REJECTED COMMERCIAL CHARACTERS

10. The Maytag Repairman Who's So Lonely He's Found Swinging from the Rafters

9. Blackie, the Oil-Soaked Exxon Seagull

8. Roadkill Ralph, the Goodyear Tire Mascot

7. Mr. Peanut for Calvin Klein Underwear

6. Jitters, the Chase & Sanborn Caffeine Hound

5. Flipped-Out Mr. Zip, the Disgruntled Post Office Employee

4. NutraSweet Pete, the Hairless Lab Rat

3. Greyhound Gus, the Bus-Riding Drifter

2. Daniel Patrick Moynihan, the Lucky Charms Senator

1. Anatomically Correct Poppin' Fresh

TOP TEN WAYS TO SPEED UP OUR JUSTICE SYSTEM

10. Cut week-long "going away" parties for dismissed jurors

9. Just have Monty Hall come in and let defendant pick which curtain has freedom, jail, or a big donkey

8. Drive-thru courtrooms

7. Let people say "Y'honor" instead of "Your Honor"

6. Each time a case is wrapped up, every lawyer involved gets a fresh-baked Toll House cookie

5. New rule: Blink on the stand—go to jail

4. Eliminate the production numbers—nobody likes them anyway

3. Bailiffs on Dexedrine

2. Settle our disputes the way the Founding Fathers intended: In the Atlasphere

1. *Adiós,* Trial by One's Peers; *Buenos Días,* Coin Toss

TOP TEN CANADIAN COMPLAINTS ABOUT AMERICAN TV

10. Whenever they show Niagara Falls, always "happens" to be on the U.S. side

9. No *Monday Night Curling*

8. *Friends* theme song makes Sasquatch go loco

7. You can watch MTV for a week and not see a single Gordon Lightfoot video

6. During *Cheers* reruns, real beer should pour out of the TV

5. Not enough exciting canoe chases

4. How about more smutty double entendres using the word *Saskatoon*?

3. *ER* never about frostbite

2. Too much Dave. Not enough Paul.

1. It's really hard to play along with *Jeopardy* after you've drunk a couple dozen Molsons

TOP TEN SIGNS YOU SMOKE TOO MUCH

10. In the middle of smoking a cigarette, you pause for a "cigarette break"

9. Your birthday is a state holiday in North Carolina

8. Your title for the Surgeon General: "Captain Bringdown"

7. Cracking your knuckles leaves you winded

6. Morning schedule: Wake up, cough for three hours, take nap

5. In your neighborhood, they give directions by saying "Go down to the big pile of cigarette butts . . ."

4. You get mattress fires more often than you do haircuts

3. You smoke *during* sex

2. You refer to nonsmokers as "pink-lunged sissy boys"

1. You explain to nurse you didn't realize you were in a "nonsmoking" iron lung

TOP TEN CHANGES IF THE U.S.A. WERE OWNED BY DISNEY

10. Just like cows in India, sacred mice would wander freely through the streets

9. Delaware, Maryland, and Rhode Island renamed "Huey," "Louie," and "Dewey"

8. Emergency-vehicle sirens would blast Donald Duck gibberish

7. Winning athletes exclaim, "I'm going to any random spot in the country!"

6. Impact of bad economic news softened by having it announced by Goofy

5. Instead of death penalty, convicted killers must listen to "It's a Small World After All" for the rest of their lives

4. *The* Mickey Mouse president, instead of *a* Mickey Mouse president

3. The nation's sidewalks run with dalmatian urine

2. *"Put the black rubber nose back on, you fool, or the secret police will haul you off to the gulag!"*

1. We'd bomb Busch Gardens back to the Stone Age

TOP TEN REASONS LIZ TAYLOR IS DIVORCING LARRY FORTENSKY

10. The liquor and pills finally wore off

9. Only common interest was eating mayonnaise straight out of the jar

8. He kept asking for increases in his allowance

7. The "ungodly stench" he complained of turned out to be her latest fragrance

6. He dozed off during their tenth daily screening of *National Velvet*

5. Every time they had sex, she'd need a new hip

4. It dawned on her that she was married to *Larry Fortensky*

3. She traded him to Zsa Zsa for $500,000 and two future draft picks

2. She's fallen in love with another man that she wants to marry and then divorce

1. Only one way for her to stay in business: *Volume, volume, volume!*

TOP TEN SIGNS DICK VITALE IS NUTS

10. Stands during national anthem—
    on his head

 9. Right before every jump ball, claims to
    hear the basketball whispering his name

 8. For a cheap rush, takes hits of stale air
    from old basketballs

 7. Sleeps on a pile of shattered backboards

 6. Was 33 before he figured out the
    Globetrotters games were rigged

 5. Ongoing campaign to get his bathrobe
    inducted into the Hall of Fame

 4. His sleeper team in the final four:
    The Judds

 3. Has an irrational fear of the possession
    arrow

 2. Moments after his first child was born,
    dumped Gatorade on his wife

 1. Likes to run through locker rooms wearing
    nothing but a referee's whistle yelling
    "BABY!"

TOP TEN WAYS TO IMPROVE THE RATINGS OF *60 MINUTES*

10. More on-air patter about how "horny" everyone is

9. "Rachel Cut" for Mike Wallace

8. Impose a two-minute limit to Morley Safer's harp solos

7. More hard-hitting exposés on corruption in the lapdancing industry

6. Have Ed Bradlee add a couple more *E*'s to his name

5. Add wacky next-door neighbor played by Don Knotts

4. Bring in Howard Stern to cover lesbian beat

3. Before Andy Rooney does his segment, have him down a pint of schnapps

2. Once per show, camera crew bursts in on someone just getting out of the shower

1. Correspondent kickline at end of the hour

TOP TEN SIGNS YOUR WIFE IS HAVING AN AFFAIR WITH PRINCE CHARLES

10. Hidden in the closet, you find a pair of earmuffs the size of Frisbees

9. Her unemployed brother suddenly gets a job as a viscount

8. Constantly asking why you can't be more of a dweeb

7. Her old hobby: Collecting *TV Guide*s
   Her new hobby: Polo

6. You hear her on the phone giggling, "Yeah, the idiot has to work for a living"

5. You get a call from Buckingham Palace asking you to come pick up your wife's bra

4. You leave the toilet seat up and she threatens to have you beheaded

3. Her new wall plaque: OFFICIAL SUPPLIER OF SEX TO HIS ROYAL HIGHNESS, THE PRINCE OF WALES

2. Has no plausible explanation for why her face is on the five-pound note

1. The crown marks on her thighs

TOP TEN THINGS O.J. DID THE DAY AFTER THE VERDICT

10. Planted bloody "thank you" note at Mark Fuhrman's place

9. Reprimanded Kato for leaving Jacuzzi running for an entire year

8. Told J. Crew to start sending catalogs to home again

7. Talked to Hallmark about a line of "race cards"

6. Made Al Cowlings laugh by finally trying on the fake beard in the glove compartment

5. Long-shot call to Hertz

4. Unpacked 14 new porcelain kitties from the Porcelain Kitty of the Month Club

3. Bought new gloves

2. Got out hedge clippers to really "O.J." those hedges!

1. Pinched himself

TOP TEN THINGS OVERHEARD AT THE WORLD CONFERENCE FOR WOMEN

10. "*You* used to date Martina? *I* used to date Martina!"

9. "If one more person offers me some General Foods International Coffee, I swear I'm gonna puke."

8. "The customs officials seem confused by RuPaul's passport."

7. "Ooooh! Look at the Big Serious Feminist smoking Virginia Slims!"

6. "Hillary's upset because she just called the White House and Gennifer Flowers answered."

5. "I can't wait for the keynote address from Hef."

4. "Are the men gone? Okay—bring out the Tupperware!"

3. "Which way to Leona Helmsley's Bitch Seminar?"

2. "Hey, Mrs. Mandela! Quit hogging the cookie dough!"

1. "It's simple: Women *have* boobs. Men *are* boobs."

TOP TEN SIGNS H & R BLOCK HAVE GONE INSANE

10. For two extra deductions, they demand you adopt them

9. Insist there's no such number as "4"

8. To make your tax appointment, you have to shoot your way into their fortified compound

7. Howl like coyotes whenever they see a W-2

6. Advise you to take your refund in giant stone coins from the Micronesian isle of Yap

5. Sign all documents with bloody handprints

4. On difficult questions, they ask advice from a mannequin wearing an Uncle Sam costume

3. Sprinkle your return with "anti-audit juice"

2. Tell you to skip paying taxes because the world is going to end in the year 2000 anyway

1. After finishing your return, they celebrate by stripping down to their underpants and making you some eggs

TOP TEN REJECTED SLOGANS FOR FORD

10. "Where quality is job . . . what, maybe 5 . . . or 6"

9. "You might be a big class-action winner!"

8. "Ford: Because life is too predictable"

7. "Our cars are built with love because our assembly-line workers enjoy unlimited cocktails"

6. "One out of every 50 glove compartments contains an abandoned newborn!"

5. "Turn the key; cross your fingers"

4. "They may be fiery death traps, but they're *American-made* fiery death traps!"

3. "If you have a better idea, could you send it to us?"

2. "You know how they say you should live every day as if it's your last?"

1. "Wouldn't you rather take the bus?"

Trooper First Class John Barone.
Met Dave September 15, 1995.

Sergeant Bernard
Moncrief.
Met Dave
July 26, 1991.

Trooper First Class Robert Burke. Met
Dave May 2, 1995.

Trooper First Class
Conrad Winalski. Met
Dave September 15,
1995, with TFC John
Barone.

Trooper First Class Michael Smarz.
Met Dave November 27, 1994.

Trooper First Class
Wilfredo Mercado. Met
Dave June 11, 1993.

Trooper First Class Vito F. Savino. Met Dave October 2, 1985.

Trooper First Class Debbie Roy. Met Dave
February 27, 1996. The canned ham was a gift
from Mr. Letterman.

Trooper First Class Scott
Harvey. Met Dave
June 14, 1995.

Trooper First Class Joseph Marchio. Met Dave
September 9, 1992.

Trooper First Class Kenneth Rigney. Met Dave May 17, 1995. The canned ham was not a gift from Mr. Letterman.

Trooper First Class Paul Galietti. Met Dave July 19, 1992.

Trooper First Class Eric
Breuer. Met Dave
April 12, 1996.

Steve Young's
Uncle Bobby.

TOP TEN LITTLE-KNOWN FACTS ABOUT COLIN POWELL

10. Arranges his peas in parade formation before eating them

9. Originally tried to name military campaign in the Persian Gulf after his favorite movie: Operation *Breakfast at Tiffany's*

8. College fraternity nickname: Staff Chief of Joints

7. Hardly fits in his car what with all the empty Mountain Dew bottles and crumpled-up lottery tickets

6. Conducted some unusual wind-tunnel tests with Divine Brown

5. He and Schwarzkopf have signed to costar in *Lethal Weapon IV*

4. Doesn't ask; doesn't tell

3. His real ambition: To be the seventh "Friend"

2. Favorite pickup line: "I'd like to do more to you by 9 A.M. than most people do all day"

1. Streisand freak

DAVE LETTERMAN'S TOP TEN EXCUSES FOR NOT WINNING AN EMMY AWARD

10. "Only been giving 109 percent"

9. "Did away with our old category: Shows That Suck Big Time"

8. "Bad press since I strangled that heckler in the balcony"

7. "Show's constant high-pitched hum drove the judges nuts"

6. "Mistakenly tried to impress the *Merchant Marine* Academy"

5. "Been consistently snubbed ever since I made *Yentl*"

4. "Many viewers sickened by my raw-meat neckties"

3. "Ever since I developed Tourette's syndrome, the show has been more sad than funny"

2. "We actually did win, but the band failed the drug test"

1. "Guess they've seen the show"

TOP TEN ERRORS IN THE MOVIE *APOLLO 13*

10. Real *Apollo 13* never picked up a hitchhiking E.T.

9. To fix spacecraft, Tom Hanks just hits it like The Fonz

8. No record of Jim Lovell telling Houston, "Forget about us! Just free Willy!"

7. Character played by Kevin Bacon was actually a rhesus monkey

6. In reality, astronauts' wives did not hang around Mission Control topless

5. No historical basis for moon being covered with giant Taco Bell logo

4. U.S. president in 1970 was Richard Nixon, not Thomas Jefferson

3. On-board sundae bar not introduced until Skylab

2. Of the three real crew members, none was a Klingon

1. Nobody actually had to get out and push

TOP TEN GOOD THINGS ABOUT BEING MARRIED TO CLINT EASTWOOD

10. Those romantic Sunday afternoons spent blowing away lowlifes

9. Satisfaction of knowing your husband is the world's squintiest guy

8. If your pizza isn't there in 30 minutes, the delivery guy is a dead man

7. Your three lovely children: Dirty Larry, Dirty Mary, and Dirty Gary

6. His charming insistence that the words *"Do you feel lucky, punk?"* be incorporated into wedding vows

5. Has hundreds of great stories about working with orangutan

4. Get to "do it" under every bridge in Madison County

3. The man can sing!

2. If marriage doesn't work out, you can count on him for a fistful of alimony

1. Turns out, in all those movies, that *wasn't* a gun in his pocket

TOP TEN THINGS BILL CLINTON DOES TO ANNOY NEWT GINGRICH

10. Has pilot do barrel rolls when Newt is in the Air Force One bathroom

9. Every Christmas, gives him a 55-gallon drum of Grecian Formula

8. Sends squad of navy Seals to give him a pink belly

7. Doesn't even bother making a pass at his wife

6. Sucker-punches him right in the gingrich

5. Won't let him have any of the cool office supplies that Hillary stole from Vince Foster's desk

4. Whoopee cushion on Speaker's chair

3. At harpsichord recitals, slips off one of his perfumed gloves and slaps Newt right across his beauty spot

2. Tells him, "I can't inhale—until you have a Certs"

1. Teases him about his tiny gavel

TOP TEN LIFEGUARD PICKUP LINES

10. "Has anyone ever told you how beautiful you look coughing seawater out of your lungs?"

9. "Can I buy you a glass of Coppertone?"

8. "Will you help me anchor my lifeguard tower by sitting in my lap?"

7. "If I can't have you, life isn't worth guarding."

6. "Let's go someplace quiet for some running and horseplay."

5. "My friend and I have a bet: Are you drowning?"

4. "As far as I'm concerned, you can go ahead and piss in the pool."

3. "I want to be with you tonight—even if you are a plastic CPR training dummy."

2. "How about slipping out of those wet things and into a dry martini?"

1. "The surf isn't the only thing that's up."

TOP TEN SHOCKING ITEMS IN THE LATEST ISSUE OF *CONSUMER REPORTS*

10. Steer clear of the new Cardboard Chrysler

9. Them cookie-baking Keebler elves almost never wash their hands

8. After their Nighttime Formula Cough Suppressant has you sleeping soundly, the guys from NyQuil back a truck up to your house and empty it out

7. Frank Perdue might be "doing it" with some of the larger oven roasters

6. Hohner harmonicas are all tested by a guy with a wet, hacking cough

5. While no scientific corollary has been officially established, the people who drink Yoo-Hoo tend to be morons

4. Continued exposure to Uncle Ben's rice may induce a vague sense of liberal guilt

3. While no one doesn't like her, Sara Lee is a hateful, right-wing bigot who doesn't like anyone else

2. A lot of the scenes they show on the side of the porno videotape box aren't even in the damn movie!

1. Those guys over at Underwriters Laboratories are a bunch of wussies!

TOP TEN WAYS SUPREME COURT JUSTICES UNWIND

10. Take gavel to amusement park and go nuts on the "Whack-a-Mole" game

9. Hit the beach to lose those "robe lines"

8. Play the Vatican in softball

7. Sit around restaurant ruling on "Folgers Crystals vs. Coffee Normally Served There"

6. Drop by lower courts, order rookie judges to "drop and give me twenty"

5. Knock back a couple of Supreme brewskis; fall asleep on the Supreme couch

4. Prank calls to Roe, pretending to be Wade

3. Antiquing with a favorite bailiff

2. Hang around Bureau of Alcohol, Tobacco and Firearms; drink, smoke, and shoot off guns

1. Get it on with a couple of jurisprudence groupies

TOP TEN EXCUSES FOR SUCKING AT TENNIS

10. Thought I was playing mixed doubles; depended too much on my imaginary friend

9. Should've brought own shoes instead of renting

8. Too much Riunite and Gatorade

7. Thought match was best 17 out of 33

6. Hard to play well when your Psychic Friend has told you she just doesn't see you winning

5. Shouldn't have restrung racket with Andre Agassi's old ponytail

4. Kept hoping the federal government would bail me out

3. I fell for the old "let's see who can hit the ball softer" line

2. Did I mention the Curse of King Tut's Tomb, which, thank God, only afflicts my family in their leisure-time activities?

1. *Dang!* Them tennis balls is awful bouncy!

TOP TEN THINGS OVERHEARD IN TIMES SQUARE ON NEW YEAR'S EVE

10. "I'm a New York public-school graduate—what comes after 10, 9, 8?"

9. "*Awww*, look! Rats with little party hats!"

8. "At the stroke of midnight, you can watch my pants drop."

7. "Wow! Almost as much vomit as St. Patrick's Day."

6. "Look at the fine detail, the craftsmanship . . . Dick Clark's face is just amazing!"

5. "How much are the 9mm 'noisemakers'?"

4. "I'm not picking your pocket—I'm just lonely."

3. "Please, *please* tell me that isn't Al Sharpton in a diaper."

2. "It's crowded! It's disorderly! It stinks! Just like the rest of the year!"

1. "Uh-oh. That ain't champagne."

TOP TEN PROPOSED CHANGES IN THE RULES OF BASEBALL

10. Instead of 162 games a season, one game with 162 guys on each side

9. The runner is also out if fielder can hit him with a gob of chewing tobacco

8. Glass bats full of tapioca

7. If catcher snags your pop foul, he gets to make out with your wife in the stands for a while

6. Extra outs for every person on team named "Mookie," "Scooter," or "Pee Wee"

5. Outfield crowded with hundreds of honking, irritable geese

4. Instead of leather mitts, big fluffy handfuls of Reddi Wip

3. Three strikes and you're out! No kidding! As in *life imprisonment*!

2. Switch hitters must be bisexual

1. Reach a base, do a shot

TOP TEN LOUSIEST JOBS

10. Lifeguard at the Sewage Treatment Plant

9. Door-to-Door Live Walrus Salesman

8. Street Mime in the South Bronx

7. Freelance Speed Bump

6. Bill Collector for Dr. Kevorkian

5. On-Set Tutor, *Hee Haw*

4. Guy at One-Hour Photo Place Who Has to Develop Roseanne's Birthing Photos

3. Minority Recruiter, Aryan Nation

2. Dunk-Tank Clown in Roger Clemens's hometown

1. Spotter, Fat Guy Olympics

TOP TEN EXCUSES FOR LOSING AN ELECTION

10. Shouldn't have delivered all my campaign speeches in Esperanto

9. Low turnout among my strongest supporters: Preschoolers and the recently deceased

8. Didn't know camera was on when I took a leak behind podium

7. Should've kept quiet about seeing *Hello, Dolly!* 63 times

6. Misread memo advising me to "kiss babies" as "kiss babes"

5. Maybe cutting off all my shirts to expose my midriff wasn't such a great idea

4. Accidentally released negative campaign ads about myself

3. Big mistake: Proving I'm not a racist by doing my adorable "Buckwheat" character

2. Uninspired slogan: "Vote for Me If You Get a Chance"

1. Wanted to campaign, but couldn't tear myself away from Must See TV

TOP TEN SIGNS YOU HAVE GAMBLING FEVER

10. You've got a pool going on the exact date your aunt Helen will pass away

9. When they pass the collection plate at church, you ask, "What kind of odds am I getting?"

8. In produce section of supermarket, you point and say, "Look—those things from the little slot-machine windows!"

7. You're wearing green felt underpants

6. You get Christmas cards from Siegfried & Roy

5. For luck, you've got a whole dead rabbit on your key chain

4. You've asked your boss for an eleven-year advance on your salary

3. Named your kids "Tropicana," "Sahara," and "Circus Circus"

2. Wife wonders why you keep coming home with broken legs

1. Two words: Roulette rash

TOP TEN THINGS MADONNA IS LOOKING FOR IN A HUSBAND

10. Ability to "vogue" while pushing a lawn mower

9. Someone who will be patient while she's in the bathroom reinventing herself

8. Knowing how to nicely explain to the kids that "Mommy's out hitchhiking naked for a while"

7. Opposable thumbs

6. Willingness to raise daughter as a foulmouthed tramp

5. A steady nine-to-five job and must make at least $27,000 a year

4. While watching NBA game together, shouldn't mind Madonna saying, *"Did him, did him, did him, want him, did him . . ."*

3. Agrees that if she catches him with a mistress, he has to let her in on it

2. It helps if you're not Sean Penn

1. Must have experience operating a cone bra

TOP TEN LEAST POPULAR CHRISTMAS CAROLS

10. "Rudolph the Reindeer with an Inner Ear Disorder"

9. "Joy to the World Wrestling Federation"

8. "Away in a Drunk Tank"

7. "Here We Come A-Wassailing, Whatever the Hell That Means"

6. "It's Beginning to Look a Lot Infected"

5. "Deck the Halls with No-Pest Strips"

4. "Frosty the Pedophile"

3. "Have a Super-Duper Okie-Dokey Kwanza"

2. "Jack Frost Roasting on an Open Fire"

1. "Walking in a Woman's Wonderbra"

TOP TEN THINGS ON CLINTON'S CAMPAIGN "TO DO" LIST

10. Promise the American people second term won't suck as bad as the first

9. See if Paula Jones will drop charges if offered the vice presidency

8. Sample as many flavors of cake as possible; eventually pick an official "Campaign Cake"

7. Boating trip with Roger. Make it look like accident.

6. Dig up another totally lame Fleetwood Mac song

5. Reach out to largest bloc of voters—the millions of failed cabinet nominees

4. Start slipping acid into Perot's coffee again

3. Teach Socks to do that "chow-chow-chow" dance; the voters will *love* it!

2. Teach Warren Christopher to do that "chow-chow-chow" dance; the voters will *love* it!

1. Let evil robot masters from the future know that the nation's been completely fouled up—*exactly according to plan!*

TOP TEN SIGNS THAT MAYBE CAL RIPKEN SHOULD TAKE A DAY OFF AFTER ALL

10. To avoid missing game, recently removed own appendix during seventh-inning stretch

9. His infield chatter consists of "Man, I'm tired. Man, I'm tired. Man, I'm tired. . . ."

8. Covered head to toe with a rash that looks like baseball stitching

7. Occasionally does interpretive dance to "The Star-Spangled Banner"

6. Believes Marv Albert is trying to sabotage him by telepathically sending him "evil blooper vibrations"

5. While signing autographs, has been asking fans, "What's my name again?"

4. Frequently moved to tears by what he calls the "miracle of ballpark franks plumping"

3. Instead of cleats, sometimes wears pink bunny slippers

2. Can only communicate with family and friends through coaching signs

1. Keeps flipping crowd "the Oriole"

TOP TEN LITTLE-KNOWN FACTS ABOUT PRINCESS DIANA

10. Wants to be called "The Artist Formerly Known As Princess"

9. Once screamed at Elizabeth II, "Who died and made you queen?"

8. While visiting New York last year, lost a diamond-encrusted tiara at a sidewalk three-card monte game

7. Works nights at Euro-Hooters

6. Prince Charles once urged her to get ear implants

5. Has had sexual relations with most of the wax figures at Madame Tussaud's

4. Actually has a GTE Princess phone

3. Has challenged Camilla Parker-Bowles to a Pay-Per-View "Extreme Fighting" match

2. Yes, James Hewitt was in the "double digits"—but remember, they use the metric system

1. Loves the fish; can't stand the chips

TOP TEN REJECTED NEW YORK CITY TOURIST SLOGANS

10. "Visit the Big Apple or We'll Beat You into a Coma"

9. "Stop and Smell the Hudson"

8. "New York: A Steaming Pile of Fun!"

7. "Think of It As Sea World with Lots of Floating Mob Informants"

6. "Now with Monthly Garbage Pickup!"

5. "You'll Come for the Sights; You'll Stay for the Police Lineup!"

4. "We Don't Need No Stinkin' Arch"

3. "Take a Free Swing at Anybody Who Looks at You Funny"

2. "Washington, We Have a Problem"

1. "We Can Kick Your City's Ass"

TOP TEN LARRY KING PICKUP LINES

10. "I want to make you my Larry Queen."

9. "I learned everything I know about the ladies from that crazy little love monkey, Ross Perot."

8. "You've got all the good qualities of wives four and six *combined*!"

7. "I'm the closest you'll ever get to kissing Brando."

6. "Let's get out of this soundproof radio booth and go someplace quiet where we can talk."

5. "Looking at you really puts a strain on my suspenders, if you know what I mean."

4. "How'd you like to get a gratuitous mention in my column?"

3. "I've never been attracted to a man before, Mr. Vice President."

2. "Wanna 'simulcast'?"

1. "Haven't I married you someplace before?"

TOP TEN LEAST POPULAR NEW GROCERY PRODUCTS

10. Jockey Brand Roast Poultry in Briefs

9. Little-Debbie-with-the-Mumps Snack Cakes

8. Sears Kem-Tone Cake Frosting

7. *Whoopsie!* Brand Sausage Bloopers

6. Stokely's Highly Poisonous Mushrooms in Sauce (*for decorative purposes only*)

5. Manhattan Clam Chowder with Real Manhattan "Clams"

4. Batter-Dipped Whole Pigeon on a Stick

3. Birds Eye Frozen Lawn Clippings

2. Skoal Baby Food

1. Mrs. Butterworth's Maple-Flavored Birth-Control Syrup

TOP TEN SIGNS YOU'RE ADDICTED TO TV FOOTBALL

10. You get absolutely no sleep the night before the Jeep Eagle Aloha Bowl

9. To feel closer to some of your favorite players, you tear the cartilage in your knee

8. Most humans: 75 percent water.
   You: 75 percent chip dip

7. Couple times a day, you use the expression "time to drain the Dierdorf"

6. You pay $22 million to have Deion Sanders shovel your driveway

5. Your retinas are crisscrossed with telestrator burns

4. You only watch *Live with Regis and Kathie Lee* to hear stories about Frank

3. Spent your family's savings to have actual pigskin painfully grafted onto 90 percent of your body

2. You've been banned from the A & P for spiking melons

1. You tell the paramedic attaching the defibrillator to your chest to get the hell out of the way of the TV screen

TOP TEN SUPERMODEL COMPLAINTS ABOUT MEN

10. Ever since David Copperfield hooked up with Claudia Schiffer, dweebs keep trying to pull quarters out of your ear

9. They keep using lame pickup lines like "C'mon, let's do it right here on the Oval Office desk!"

8. Constantly having to say, "Thanks, Einstein—I *am* a model!"

7. How the mailman always brings your mail right into the shower

6. When they tell you your swimsuit work was "very important" to them in prison

5. Suggestions that you get mole implants

4. They look at you funny when you eat Crisco right out of the can

3. All that talk talk talk—when all we really want to do is have sex

2. When they run out of snacks and start eating your birth-control pills

1. Sometimes big feet just means big feet

TOP TEN SIGNS YOU'RE NOT ONE OF *TIME* MAGAZINE'S "25 MOST INFLUENTIAL PEOPLE IN AMERICA"

10. When you tell bus drivers, "This is my stop," they always say, "So?"

9. You're 50 years old and you still share a bunk bed with your brother

8. The Nielsen ratings company informs you that nobody gives a good goddamn what you watch

7. You: "Happy Mother's Day, Mom!"
Your mom: "Do I know you?"

6. Houseflies don't budge when you wave your hands near them

5. You discover a new comet, but the scientific community decides to call it "Seinfeld's Comet"

4. You're the first thing seen by a nestful of hatching chicks, but they just don't consider you mother material

3. You're president of Americans for the Metric System

2. Your best pickup line: "Want to see my freshly washed Ford Fiesta?"

1. You're listed in *Who's Not Who*

TOP TEN ITEMS ON O.J.'S LEGAL BILL

10. One Rhyming Dictionary for Johnnie Cochran

9. One Jumbo Jar of Hand-Swelling Cream

8. Overnight Service: Kardashian's Laundry

7. Subliminal "Not Guilty" Cuff Links Worn by Barry Scheck

6. Three Cans of Eyebrow Mousse for Robert Shapiro

5. Ten Copies: *1001 Ways to Hypnotize a Jury*

4. F. Lee Bailey's Million-Dollar "Refreshment Fee"

3. Conjugal Visits with Various Briefcases

2. Gas to Keep Bronco Idling in Front of Courthouse for 15 Months

1. Cake with File in It (Unused)

TOP TEN NEW ITEMS IN THE KATHIE LEE GIFFORD PRODUCT LINE

10. "Carnival Booze" Malt Liquor

9. Cody 'n Cassidy Salt-and-Pepper Shakers

8. *Eau de Frank* Designer Fragrance for Men

7. "World's Greatest Mom" Frozen TV Dinners

6. "Chatty Kathie Lee" Endlessly Talking Dolls

5. "If They Could See Me Now" Religious Conversion Kit

4. "Talk Like Regis" Brand Amphetamines

3. Add-a-Lee Prosthetic Middle Name

2. *Christmas in the Tropics* CD with Kathie Lee and the Honduran Sweatshop Children's Chorus

1. Desk Calendar with 365 Synonyms for "Perky"

TOP TEN BIKER PICKUP LINES

10. "Mmm, you smell like Quaker State."

9. "Wanna see my kickstand?"

8. "Anybody you want stomped?"

7. "I've done it with both Harley and Davidson."

6. "Am I dreaming or do you appear to have most of your teeth?"

5. "I'll show you my tattoos if you show me yours."

4. "Looking at you makes me forget I'm burning my ankle on the exhaust pipe."

3. "Is it love—or am I loopy on carbon monoxide?"

2. "Excuse me, are you wearing Windsong by Prince Matchabelli?"

1. "You ain't a cop, are you?"

TOP TEN SIGNS YOU HAVE A BAD PSYCHIC ADVISER

10. At your first session she asks, "Are you here for a séance or a massage?"

9. Urges you to get in touch with the "real Bob" inside you, but your name's Walter

8. Keeps slapping down tarot cards and shouting *"Gin!"*

7. Answers all your questions with, "Hold on while I ask LaToya"

6. For the last five years running, has predicted the Mets will "go all the way"

5. Says, "You will soon be the victim of a hilarious practical joke," then squirts ketchup on your pants

4. For $5,000, she tells you what movies will be opening on Friday

3. Her crystal ball has three finger holes in it

2. Only accurate prediction was that your parking meter was about to expire

1. Has a vision in which you're ripped off by someone who looks just like her

TOP TEN GOOD THINGS ABOUT BEING IN THE NAVY

10. You can say "ahoy" without sounding like a total dweeb

9. Seasickness is a great way to keep the weight off

8. If an old sneaker floats past you in the water and you can snag it, it's yours

7. Get in free to Village People concerts

6. Skeet shooting old Buicks with deck catapult and 35mm cannon

5. Bitchin' hats

4. If anybody gives you a hard time, you just down a can of spinach and beat the crap out of 'em

3. Barnacles make surprisingly good pets

2. Shitloads of taffy

1. Exotic ports, exotic women, exotic rashes

TOP TEN WAYS HILLARY CLINTON COULD IMPROVE HER IMAGE

10. Propose health-care plan that relies on the therapeutic properties of ice-cold Budweiser

9. After Chief of Staff Leon Panetta "accidentally" falls down an old abandoned well, she climbs down and rescues him

8. Appear on Broadway for a couple months playing Rizzo in *Grease*

7. Series of daring gas-station holdups across the Midwest

6. Have laser surgery to remove the "666" from her scalp

5. Become celebrity spokesperson for Sara Lee, because nobody doesn't like Sara Lee!

4. After president's weekly radio address, she comes on to make a hilarious prank phone call

3. On Blockbuster videos, right after FBI warning about not copying them, insert shot of her rolling her eyes and saying "Yeah, right"

2. Go away for about 10 to 12 years

1. Stop wearing the "I'm with Stupid" T-shirt

TOP TEN SIGNS IT'S COLD IN NEW YORK CITY

10. Dramatic increase in icicle-related homicides

9. Pedestrians buying hot roasted chestnuts to put in their pants

8. Instead of the finger, New Yorkers giving each other the mitten

7. Flashers exposing themselves much more briefly

6. A lot of people in ski masks who aren't necessarily bank robbers

5. Canned sodas sold with street hot dogs have gone from lukewarm to tepid

4. Eddie Bauer store experiencing marked upswing in shoplifting

3. World Trade towers huddled together for warmth

2. Emergency rooms packed with guys whose tongues have frozen to hookers

1. Cabbies wearing flannel turbans

TOP TEN WAYS MAJOR LEAGUE BASEBALL CAN WIN BACK THE FANS

10. New rule: Catch a foul ball, win the salary of the guy who hit it

9. Whole team has to play entire game squatting like the catcher

8. Install a TV monitor at every seat so fans can watch something else

7. Nine players, eight uniforms

6. Players can't do drugs unless they bring enough to go around

5. Get Michael Jordan back and change rules to include inflatable ball, wood floors, and a hoop with a net

4. Remember Babe Ruth? Well, how's about some more of them ballplayin' fat dudes?

3. Opposing team mascots face off in switchblade fights

2. At first base, the runner has to *kiss* the first baseman. At second base . . . Well, you get the idea

1. Shower with the Players Night

TOP TEN LEAST POPULAR ITEMS AT THE DISNEY STORE

10. Mickey Mouse Glue Traps

9. *101 Dalmatians* Birth-Control Pills

8. "The Visible Goofy" Educational Figure

7. Chocolate-Covered Jiminy Crickets

6. "It's a Small World" Boxer Shorts

5. Rabid Pluto Foaming Cappuccino Maker

4. Sneezy Doll with Runny-Nose Action

3. Aladdin's Two-in-One Lamp and Crack Pipe

2. XXX Cartoon: *Chip Does Dale*

1. Cryogenic Frozen Waltsicles

TOP TEN AGREEMENTS REACHED BY CLINTON AND YELTSIN

10. Russia will resume making payments on Girl Scout cookies ordered from Chelsea

9. Agree to disagree on who's puffier

8. By mid–1997, through unilateral efforts, the gradual phasing back in of that monkey character on *Friends*

7. If Quebec does secede from Canada, it will be a *really obnoxious* country

6. Beer before liquor, get drunk quicker

5. That blond diplomatic attaché from Sweden: *Yowzah!*

4. Whopper with cheese costs more than plain Whopper, but worth it

3. Opening next year: Disney Worldski

2. If a terrorist put a gun to your head and forced you to kiss a guy, guess you'd have to go with Antonio Banderas

1. Vodka. French fries. The potato is God's greatest creation.

TOP TEN SHOCKING SECRETS OF THE MUSIC INDUSTRY

10. Under his big hat, Garth Brooks has a world-class mushroom farm

9. "Weird Al" Yankovic had his name legally changed from "Odd Bob" Johnson

8. Ice-T's controversial "Cop Killer" song was originally written for Carol Channing to perform in the show *Hello, Dolly!*

7. The last 101 Strings album was recorded using only 97 strings

6. Kenny Rogers does not in fact have the slightest idea when to hold 'em or when to fold 'em

5. That Captain guy of the Captain and Tennille isn't even a real captain

4. For the last couple of years, Paul and Mary have been pretty much carrying Peter

3. Ever listen to Dan Fogelberg? Did you know he's a *white guy*?!

2. Unknown to most of her fans worldwide, tambourine great Linda McCartney is quietly married to a guy named Paul McCartney

1. The Village People? Straight as arrows, every man jack of 'em!

TOP TEN SIGNS YOU'RE AT A BAD PARTY

10. Instead of a sound system, they've rigged up a 130-decibel ocean-liner horn

9. All the broken hips have put a pall on the conga line

8. Prison regulations require lights out at 10:00

7. You've had eight Colt .45's and you haven't gotten it on with Billy Dee Williams yet

6. Theme: "Come As Your Favorite CPA"

5. Off-brand of champagne that comes in a resealable plastic bag

4. You're surprised to learn that Exxon makes a chip dip

3. Hostess asks, "Have you ever had monkey blood before?"

2. Cops appear at door in response to complaints from people actually *at* the party

1. Who knew Yoko Ono made so many albums?

TOP TEN DOORMAN PET PEEVES

10. Too many coat buttons when you have to take a whiz

9. Being asked to carry groceries when your degree is in Door Opening

8. When you accidentally say, "Hot enough for you?" when what you mean to say is "Cold enough for you?"

7. Lazy tenants who ask you to come up and open the door to their fridge

6. Some joker puts Vaseline on the knobs

5. When a sudden breeze makes your epaulets blow up and smack you in the face

4. People who ask, "Can you hail me a hooker?"

3. The nickname "Lobby Admiral"

2. Oliver Stone movie about us: *Lies, lies, lies!*

1. When your lips get all whistle-chafed

TOP TEN SIGNS YOUR BROTHER IS THE UNABOMBER

10. Birthday cards he gives you are all 35,000 words long

9. Whenever you ask him what he's been up to, he says, "I haven't been sending mail bombs, that's for sure!"

8. Asks Mom for her nitroglycerin recipe

7. Long-standing subscription to *Middle-Aged Virgin* magazine

6. Whenever he was somebody's Secret Santa, they'd end up missing some fingers

5. When he first saw police sketch of Unabomber, he asked you, "Am I really that fat?"

4. May 8, 1970: Becky Johnson turns him down for the prom
   May 9, 1970: Becky Johnson explodes

3. Like 96 percent of all convicted letter-bombers, his favorite musical is *Showboat*

2. His answering machine message says, "Hi, I can't come to the phone right now; I'm out plotting the destruction of the modern industrial state"

1. Asks friends to call him "Una" for short

TOP TEN GOOD THINGS ABOUT LIZ TAYLOR

10. Without her influence, Michael Jackson might have turned into a real nut

9. Has actually caught the bridal bouquet at her own reception

8. Her gripping performances in the *Star Wars* movies as Darth Vader

7. Her fragrance Black Pearls is great for breaking in a new catcher's mitt

6. Despite new replacement hip, went ahead with last summer's motorcycle jump over Snake River Canyon

5. For decades, has provided a vital shot in the arm to America's sagging wedding industry

4. One of the few legendary screen actresses who can dunk

3. Doesn't just *like* it when construction workers whistle at her—she marries them

2. Her taste for diamond rings the size of mangoes

1. Two more husbands and she's got her own Top Ten list

TOP TEN SIGNS NEW YORK CITY COPS ARE BEING MORE COURTEOUS

10. Say "please" and "thank you" when extorting protection money from local merchants

9. In addition to your one phone call, you get a lovely glass of ginger ale

8. New slogan: "The criminal is always right!"

7. Before a strip search, they take you to dinner and a movie

6. If perpetrator remembers to call *"Shotgun!,"* he can ride in front seat instead of being handcuffed in the back

5. New "Want a Bite of My Doughnut?" community outreach program

4. Not only read you your Miranda rights, but also that day's *Marmaduke* comic

3. After kicking in door, they say, "Did we come at a bad time?"

2. With each mug shot taken, you get two wallet-sized prints

1. Three words: Pine-Scented Mace

TOP TEN REJECTED HALLMARK CARDS

10. "Nobody Knows Exactly When Your Birthday Is, But I Hope It's a Good One, Boy-Raised-by-Wolves!"

9. "Have a Wonderful New Year, Neighbor, Though I Don't See How That's Possible Since You Run a Kennel in Your Trailer"

8. "Why Can't the Spirit of Halloween Be with Us All Year Long?"

7. "Thanks for the Dry Hump, Darling"

6. "The Screaming Voices in My Head Have Ordered Me to Send You This Valentine"

5. "I'm Going to Try Harder This Year Not to Vomit in Your Magazine Rack"

4. "We Don't Really Know You or Like You, but Since We Once Did Your Dry Cleaning, We've Got Your Address"

3. "Hope You Get That Holiday Crack You're Dreaming of, My Crackhead Friend"

2. "With Heartfelt Wishes As Big As Your Ass"

1. "Sorry You Freaked Out on the Eggnog, My Lactose-Intolerant Friend"

TOP TEN PET PEEVES OF THE DALLAS COWBOY CHEERLEADERS

10. When they make us run back punts during practice

9. Getting in line at the concession stand behind John Madden

8. After the crowd gives you a *C* and an *O* and a *W* and a *B* and an *O* and a *Y* and an *S* and you ask them what they have and they don't know

7. Skimpy cheerleader outfits in Green Bay in December

6. Carpal tunnel pom-pom syndrome

5. When you have to do a routine on the sidelines right where the mounted police have been stationed

4. Despite all the health warnings, our decorative fringe still made out of asbestos

3. Have to do about twenty cartwheels to get a serious buzz going

2. In the made-for-TV movie about the Dallas Cowboy Cheerleaders, you're played by Rhea Perlman

1. Have to go through motions of cheering for team, even if you've bet heavily against them

TOP TEN WAYS TO MAKE BASKETBALL MORE EXCITING

10. Ball dangerously overinflated with volatile hydrogen

9. Teams ride around court on angry llamas

8. Players must constantly shout brand name of sneaker they have an endorsement deal with

7. If a fan throws something from the stands and it goes in the basket, it counts for his team

6. Elbows sharpened to razor-keenness

5. Technical foul equals loss of possession *and* pants

4. One player is "it"; has to touch other player who then becomes "it"

3. Backboard made of saltines

2. Instead of blowing on whistles, referees must play jazzy little riffs on clarinet

1. Court constantly seesaws back and forth

TOP TEN WAYS TO GET MENTIONED IN *ENTERTAINMENT WEEKLY*

10. Summon ghost of Eleanor Roosevelt; cast her opposite Walter Matthau in next *Grumpy Old Men* movie

9. Be a highly paid butt-double on *NYPD Blue*

8. Have brief career as child star; then knock over a liquor store

7. Have affairs with Siskel and Ebert simultaneously

6. Appear in Las Vegas as America's first *Vernon* Presley impersonator

5. Have a name that is usually preceded by the words "Spanish Super-Hunk"

4. Walk out on a stormy six-week marriage to that talking Hamburger Helper hand

3. Launch a controversial Calvin Klein underwear campaign featuring provocatively posed 90-year-olds

2. Sell enough country albums to irritate hip New Yorkers

1. Pay Heidi Fleiss by check

TOP TEN LEAST POPULAR NEW MAGAZINES

10. *Stolen Car and Driver*

9. *Eleven-Fingered Young Singles*

8. *Plagiarized Short Story Review*

7. *Hairnet Fashions*

6. *Extremely Blurry Playboy*

5. *Currently Drunk News & Views*

4. *Functional Illiterate Monthly*

3. *Lactose-Intolerant Lifestyles*

2. *Standing Water Sportsman*

1. *Subscription Card Roundup*

TOP TEN SIGNS THE PRESIDENT IS ANGRY

10. Latest radio address to the nation ended with the phrase "You can all bite me"

9. Giving people on the White House tour the finger

8. Punched the side of Al Gore's head so hard he broke his hand

7. Threw half-eaten Big Mac from South Portico, beaning a Marine Band clarinetist

6. At recent Rose Garden ceremony, had Secret Service rough up some Spelling Bee champions

5. Blurted out to Roger, "Isn't it time you got, like, *a job*?"

4. When pizza was late, beat delivery boy senseless with a Yoo-Hoo bottle

3. Feverishly adds names to long list of guys he's going to slug the minute he becomes a private citizen

2. Actually talked back to Hillary

1. Every five minutes, he's threatening to bomb Mexico

TOP TEN REJECTED TOYS

10. Razor-Sharp Slinky

9. Mob-Controlled Lego Construction Kit

8. Baby's First Steak Knife from Fisher-Price

7. Hasbro's Socket Inspector

6. Red Adair's Flaming Blanket Adventure Game

5. Plutonium Night-Light

4. Dr. Kevorkian's "Let's Put Mr. Potato Head to Sleep"

3. Super-Duper Eye Gouger from Kenner

2. Leonard Maltin Action Figure

1. Barbie's Dream Cell

TOP TEN CHANGES IN THE MISS U.S.A. PAGEANT IF THE JUDGES WERE DOGS

10. Points taken off for mange

9. Response to current-events questions should include frequent use of the words *walk* and *food*

8. Winning talent: Catching Frisbee with teeth

7. Title revoked if photographs surface of winner petting a cat

6. Contestants wearing white ribbons to promote Kennel Cough Awareness

5. New sniffing competition

4. Put your money on the girl wearing the sash made of baloney

3. Rambunctious Miss Kentucky forced to wear one of those plastic cones around her neck

2. Viewers might actually recognize some of the judges

1. Winner gets a Hartz Flea & Tick tiara

TOP TEN REJECTED SEAN CONNERY MOVIE LINES

10. "Bond. James Bond. But you can call me 'Jimbo.'"

9. "They come at you with a knife, you scream like a woman and run like crazy."

8. "Pussy Galore? That's a really funny name! It could be taken the wrong way, you know what I mean? Y'know—*Pussy? Galore?*"

7. "Please don't hurt me, Goldfinger! Oh please oh please oh pretty please!"

6. "Get Darby O'Gill over here to scrape this little bastard off my shoe."

5. "Tell me, Q—could you design a gum that won't stick to most dental work?"

4. "Hey, Beavis—that was cool!"

3. "*Hic!* Tee many martoonies!"

2. "That's Double-O Seven, as in Double-A, M-C-O. Aamco: The transmission specialists!"

1. "You can kiss my black ass!"

TOP TEN THINGS OVERHEARD ON O.J.'S TRIP TO ENGLAND

10. "For the last time, A.C., they drive on the other side of the road here!"

9. "Let me get this straight: What we call *'football,'* you Americans call *'soccer.'* And what we call *'guilty,'* you call *'not guilty.'* "

8. "One adult ticket for the Jack the Ripper Museum, please."

7. "You'll only need your passport, O.J., not the fake beard and $10,000 in cash."

6. "British Airways lost my luggage—just like Robert Kardashian did!"

5. "So this Kato person just lays about doing nothing while you pay the bills? Rather like our Royal Family."

4. "So you're also claiming that Mark Fuhrman planted these minibar charges?"

3. "I wonder if he could do anything about Linda McCartney?"

2. "Bloody O.J. can't bloody get his bloody gloves on!"

1. "Elementary, my dear Watson. He did it."

TOP TEN LEAST POPULAR ITEMS IN THE CBS STORE

10. Dr. Quinn, Inflatable Woman

9. Life-size head of Mike Wallace in solid milk chocolate

8. "Cybill & Bits" dog food

7. Souvenir tee that says THIS SHIRT HAS MORE VIEWERS THAN CBS

6. *Murder, She Wrote* home-autopsy kit

5. Cupcakes sprinkled with Ed Bradley's beard trimmings

4. Letterman hairpiece car-waxing shammy

3. Old *Miami Vice* hats found in Dumpster behind the NBC store

2. Ed Sullivan

1. Morley Safer video: *How to Make Love for 60 Minutes*

TOP TEN SURPRISES IN HILLARY CLINTON'S GRAND JURY APPEARANCE

10. Asked to tell the whole truth, her response: "Whatever"

9. Her frequent denials that she knew any "Bill Clinton"

8. When that .38 fell out of her purse

7. Promised to dedicate rest of her life to tracking down "the real shredders"

6. After stumping First Lady with a tough question, Al D'Amato spiking his clipboard and doing a hot-dog dance

5. When president showed up in audience with a date

4. Instead of dressing in "believable blue," wore suit of "whopper magenta"

3. When she pulled that Sharon Stone move from *Basic Instinct*

2. Jury mesmerized by her new hypno-hairdo

1. The "Dole for President" button

TOP TEN SIGNS YOU'RE NOT AT THE REAL MILLION-MAN MARCH

10. It's just you and that Urkel guy

9. Lots of Shriners driving little cars

8. The Marge Schott T-shirt booth

7. It's held at the DMV and the "march" is moving very slowly

6. You're surrounded by people dressed as their favorite *Star Trek* character

5. Keynote speaker: Jeff Foxworthy

4. The only marcher is Lee Majors

3. Entire group is riding a really long bicycle-built-for-one-million

2. Everyone's wearing Sansabelt slacks

1. Two words: Underdog balloon

TOP TEN SIGNS YOUR BROADWAY SHOW IS GOING TO CLOSE

10. They're converting your theater lobby into a Gap

9. For the last three performances, they haven't bothered to raise the curtain

8. *New York Times* review includes the word *blows* sixty-four times

7. There are more people onstage than in the audience—*and it's a one-man show*

6. Stage manager whispers to you, "I hear they're hiring at Blimpie's"

5. On typical night, many of the boos come from cast members

4. It's Jean-Claude Van Damme's first musical

3. Last six matinee crowds were bused in from Riker's Island

2. Some of your fellow "Cats" are sold to laboratories for testing

1. Wrecking ball keeps interrupting key scenes

TOP TEN GREAT THINGS ABOUT BEING ADOPTED BY THE CLINTONS

10. Instead of an allowance, you get a slush fund

9. Great new excuse: "Mom accidentally shredded my homework"

8. You can brag, "My dad's Secret Service agents can beat up your dad"

7. If you get caught smoking pot, just tell Dad you didn't inhale—what's he going to say?

6. Want to get your nose pierced? Just show your folks a poll indicating 60 percent of voters think it's a good idea

5. Get to hang out with all those pretty "aunts" that Dad keeps bringing by the White House

4. For five bucks, Uncle Roger will buy beer for you and your buddies

3. Snacks? Oh, you'll have snacks

2. Can lead to successful later career doing whatever it is JFK Jr. does

1. Your personal "horsey": Al Gore

TOP TEN HIGHLIGHTS OF THE PAST BASEBALL SEASON

10. Steve Howe picking a runner off first base with his .357 Magnum

9. Cameras catch Jane Fonda and Ted Turner joining "the Skybox Club"

8. Albert Belle promising to hit a reporter for that kid in the hospital

7. Detroit Tigers promotion: First nine fans at ballpark get to start

6. Fox tries broadcasting team of David Duchovny and Tori Spelling

5. Successful introduction of the "Magic Fingers" pitcher's mound

4. Dennis Rodman works a White Sox game as a ball girl

3. Bill Clinton throwing out the first pitch, and then four hours later denying he had been anywhere near Camden Yards

2. Hillary Clinton contacting the ghost of Babe Ruth, who orders up a dozen hot dogs with everything

1. Yankees threaten to move; Mets threaten to play

TOP TEN SIGNS ARNOLD SCHWARZENEGGER IS GETTING OLDER

10. He's been triggering explosions with the Clapper

9. Catchphrase changed from "I'll be back" to "Oh, my back!"

8. Lately, has to nap for a few hours after bulging the veins in his neck

7. In high-speed car-chase scenes, you can see he's left his turn signal on

6. Stunt double: Wilford Brimley

5. Recently switched from steroids to Metamucil

4. His dialogue studded with phrase "Speak up, damn it!"

3. Special effects in latest movie provided by Sy Sperling

2. After day of shooting action sequences, entire set smells like Ben-Gay

1. Can now get into own movies for $3.50

TOP TEN WAYS SADDAM HUSSEIN CAN IMPROVE HIS IMAGE

10. Tour the Midwest as Tevye in *Fiddler on the Roof*

9. At every public appearance, throw handfuls of root-beer barrels

8. Do one of those celebrity dictator golf tournaments

7. Post naked pictures of himself on the Internet

6. Pay Shaquille O'Neal millions of dollars to appear in a series of slick "Shaq Loves Iraq" spots

5. Star in new sitcom *Husseinfeld*

4. Spring for a nice set of Lee Press-On Nails

3. Start doing those "time to make the doughnuts" ads again

2. Distance himself from himself

1. Launch some delicious Gummi Scuds

TOP TEN SIGNS YOUR CAMP COUNSELOR IS INSANE

10. Announces "We'll be training for two weeks—and then it's off to 'Nam!"

9. The only craft he teaches you is check forgery

8. Seems obsessed with the idea that woodland creatures are talking about him behind his back

7. Tries to start a fire by rubbing two fingers together

6. Has you make your own squirrel jerky

5. Every time he tells ghost stories around the fire, he gets scared and wets his pants

4. "Buster," his pet tick

3. In middle of conversations, frequently says "Excuse me," picks up a stone, and says "Hello?" into it

2. The Batman costume

1. On nature walk, introduces a knotty pine as his fiancée

TOP TEN LEAST POPULAR ROCK LYRICS

10. "Sorry, sweetheart—not till we're married"

9. "Yo, my man, don't forget to get your auto insurance up to date!"

8. "*Eee-yow!* Our elected officials are really where it's at!"

7. "We're all alone now, except for my tapeworm"

6. "Let's 'get down' with some home woodburning crafts"

5. "My hot mama's got a yeast infection"

4. "We're gonna watch infomercials *all night long!*"

3. "The San Diego Metroplex is certainly a pleasant place to raise a family"

2. "Hey hey, ho ho, restrictive fiscal policies by our nation's Federal Reserve have got to go"

1. "I'm gonna rock you some of the night, but then I need my rest for that job interview tomorrow"

TOP TEN GREAT THINGS ABOUT BEING MARRIED TO THE KETCHUP KING

10. Romantic evenings in front of the fireplace toasting each other with snifters of ketchup

9. 57 varieties, if you know what I mean

8. Perfect way to piss off your first husband, the Relish Czar

7. "Power table" always reserved for you at Burger King next to condiment pumps

6. You can legally beat the hell out of anyone who pronounces it "catsup"

5. Endless series of hilarious practical jokes where it looks like he's bleeding

4. From the Royal Box at the Professional Bowling Championships, it's almost like you're on the lanes!

3. Loves it when you turn him upside down and slap him on the bottom

2. Husband is third in line to throne of McDonaldland after Mayor McCheese

1. Two words: Ketchup Jacuzzi

TOP TEN LEAST POPULAR STRIPPER NAMES

10. Ginger Vitis

9. Stanley Cupps

8. Lynn Fected

7. Snapple Lady

6. H. Rose Perot

5. Sue DaFed

4. Yogi Bare-ass

3. Tuna Helper

2. Nude Gingrich

1. Tammy Lasorda

TOP TEN WAYS O.J. SIMPSON IS LOOKING FOR THE REAL KILLERS

10. Gets on white courtesy phone at airports; has them page the real killers

9. Before sinking putt, takes a good look inside the cup to make sure they aren't hiding in there

8. Dating lingerie models who are also top-notch detectives

7. Signing autographs for money—no killer can resist a good autograph signing

6. Offering reward of a free upgrade on next Hertz rental

5. Braced up box on a stick in his backyard with a carrot inside it

4. Bumper sticker on white Bronco: "Honk If You're the Real Killers"

3. Once the bad guys find out super-psychic Dionne Warwick is on the case, they'll probably turn *themselves* in!

2. All the furry little woodland creatures and birds have promised to help out their old buddy O.J.

1. Hunkering down with a phone book and a Magic 8-Ball

TOP TEN OUTRIGHT PREVARICATIONS ABOUT GOLF LEGEND ARNOLD PALMER

10. Remember that little dog Benji? Well, Arnold Palmer *killed Benji*!

9. Has kids working for gum money down in his Honduran sweatshop

8. Once owned catfish farm with partner Saddam Hussein

7. Was rooting for Baby Jessica to stay down in that well

6. Responsible for 80 to 90 percent of all forest fires

5. During World War II, made Axis propaganda broadcasts as "Tokyo Arnold"

4. Knew more about Whitewater than what he told Congress. A *lot* more.

3. He's the one who coined the phrase "surfing the net"

2. Smells funny

1. Never apologized for breaking up the Beatles

TOP TEN THINGS BOB DOLE DOES FOR FUN

10. Moonwalking to his Bing Crosby 78's

9. All-Bran daiquiris

8. Chases kids off lawn with a rake

7. Extra-long phone calls to his Psychic Friend

6. Jamming with old band mates from Earth, Wind & Fire

5. Makes collect call to Bill Clinton from a "Vince Foster," then hangs up

4. Cornfield streaking

3. Playing keepaway with Sonny Bono's hairpiece

2. Cranks up heating pad to a sultry 11

1. Cruising for chicks with Strom Thurmond

TOP TEN REJECTED
JEOPARDY CATEGORIES

10. Bad Smells of New York City

9. Famous Anteaters

8. Things That Throb

7. Words of One Letter Only

6. Mitten Esoterica

5. Pittsburgh Bus Route Numbers

4. Weird-Ass Things Foreigners Eat

3. Orifices

2. Alex Trebek's High School Nicknames

1. Tick Lore

TOP TEN SIGNS YOU'VE BEEN EATING TOO MUCH RICE-A-RONI

10. You hear about an earthquake in San Francisco and your first thought is "Oh my God! Is the Rice-A-Roni factory okay?"

9. You've named your kids "Rice" and "Roni"

8. Waitresses constantly have to tell you, "No, sir, that doesn't come with Rice-A-Roni"

7. Every Wednesday night you join a small group meeting that begins with someone saying, "My name is Bob and I've eaten too much Rice-A-Roni"

6. You've caused such a shortage of Rice-A-Roni in your town, there's now a thriving black market in Rice-A-Roni

5. Your favorite dessert: Rice-A-Roni à la mode

4. You spend a day at the Louvre in Paris and exit grumbling, "Where were the damn pictures of Rice-A-Roni?"

3. Your wife files for divorce and names the Rice-A-Roni company as a co-respondent

2. You drink a cup of hot water and expand to three times your normal size—*just like Rice-A-Roni*

1. Your will specifies that you be buried in a giant Rice-A-Roni carton

TOP TEN QUESTIONS ON THE NEW U.S. CITIZENSHIP TEST

10. Is the Statue of Liberty wearing any underwear?

9. What is the proper amount to "tip" a congressman for a favor?

8. Is America "The Great Satan" or "A Pack of Warmongering Cowboy Imperialists"? Defend your answer.

7. What's the deal with that thing on Abe Lincoln's face?

6. Which brand of peanut butter is the "peanuttiest"?

5. Would you mind being used for spare parts if one of our natural-born citizens needs a new spleen or something?

4. Señor Perot: Loco, muy loco, or *muy muy* loco?

3. Who's the black private dick who's like a sex machine to all the chicks?

2. Why don't you go back to your own country where you belong?

1. True or false: The Constitution guarantees every citizen the right to life, liberty, and surf 'n turf

DAVE LETTERMAN'S TOP TEN PLANS FOR RETIREMENT

10. Get on city bus. Ride to end of line. Change buses. Repeat.

9. Go around helping Ed McMahon deliver those giant checks

8. Every other week: Plastic surgery

7. Grouse to young people, "In my day, we had to make do with 500 channels"

6. Stop getting speeding tickets in Connecticut; start getting speeding tickets in Florida

5. Devote himself mind, body, and soul to his whittling

4. Paint an old school bus in psychedelic colors and just follow Tesh, man!

3. Write scathing exposé of that ruthless bastard Paul Shaffer

2. Finally lose his virginity

1. Return a hero to his native Peru

TOP TEN EXCITING NEW DEVELOPMENTS IN TELEVISION

10. Good-bye boring old rectangular screen; hello new pear-shaped screen!

9. Closed captioning that reveals what the actors had for lunch

8. Picture-in-picture-in-picture-in-picture-in-picture-in-picture-in-picture-in-picture-in-picture-in-picture-in-picture-in-picture-in-picture-in-picture-in-picture-in-picture

7. If you see a beer commercial that you like, touch "3" on your remote control and an ice-cold six-pack magically appears

6. Hilarious device that gives any actor or newscaster a big idiotic Swedish accent

5. C-SPAN Shopping Network lets you buy off senators and congressmen right over the phone

4. By early 1998, you'll be able to actually "smell" Bruce Boxleitner

3. Cartoons where the cat kicks the shit out of the mouse

2. Amazing knob that lets you increase or decrease the volume
   (*Note: May be available to general public soon after this book's press time*)

1. Interactive Test Pattern

TOP TEN THINGS PRESIDENT CLINTON WOULD DO IF ALIENS INVADED AMERICA

10. Lock himself in the bathroom and scream, "Lemmee know when them space monkeys is gone!"

9. Introduce himself as "Earth Chief Bubba"

8. Dust off the ol' saxophone; soothe aliens with Billy Joel's classic love song "Just the Way You Are"

7. Call White House travel office for seat on next red-eye to Oxford

6. Find out alien weaknesses by stealing their FBI files

5. Watch what moderate Republicans do. Do that.

4. Book a room at the Marriott so he can get to know the female aliens on a "one-on-one" basis

3. Inhale like a son of a bitch

2. Thank them for distracting public from his totally screwed-up administration

1. When aliens say, "Take me to your leader," Bill points to Hillary

TOP TEN THINGS OLD PEOPLE ARE SAYING ABOUT THE KIDS TODAY

10. "We lived through a depression and a world war; they lived through *The Brady Bunch* TV show and *The Brady Bunch Movie*."

9. "They stink of Snapple and Chee•tos!"

8. "I can't even take a walk in the park without getting an assful of skateboard!"

7. "They don't seem to 'dig' my 'awesome' Sansabelt slacks."

6. "We didn't need crack in our day! We had a little something called heroin."

5. "It's a shame that nice k.d. lang hasn't found the right man yet."

4. "Don't try and tell me Willard Scott doesn't play favorites!"

3. "They're not as flavorful as the kids we killed and ate thirty years ago."

2. "I keep getting Ice Cube and Ice-T mixed up!"

1. "I think today's kids are great! Now can I at least have my credit cards and photos back?"

TOP TEN ITEMS LEFT OVER FROM OTHER TOP TEN LISTS

10. Victoria's VapoSecret

9. The Unahooker

8. Order now and receive a free Baldwin brother!

7. "That's not my upholstery—*but keep on Scotchgarding!*"

6. Lyle & Erik & Ben & Jerry & the Blowfish

5. The Kraft-matic Adjustable Macaroni and Cheese bed

4. Three words: Gooned on Phonics

3. If Dennis Rodman's hair turns pink, it means you're pregnant

2. Gettin' it on with a happenin' Mennonite

1. Siskel, Ebert, and a monkey in a sombrero

A WEDDING DRESS
PATTERN FOR THE
HUSKY BRIDE

Congratulations, sizable bride-to-be, on your pending nuptials. Best of luck, also, to those for whom this pattern will be adapted for costume parties and/or theatrical presentations in prisons or POW camps. The design is flexible, including options for a gown with sleeves (recommended for the Rubenesque Husky) and without sleeves (recommended for the Amazonian Muscular Husky).

The size 16 pattern is reproduced here in 1" scale.

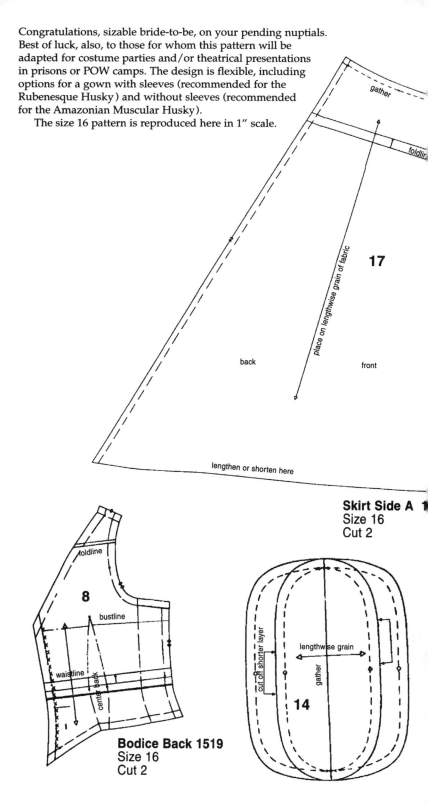

Skirt Side A 1
Size 16
Cut 2

Bodice Back 1519
Size 16
Cut 2

Sleeve Stiffening 15
Size 16
Cut 2

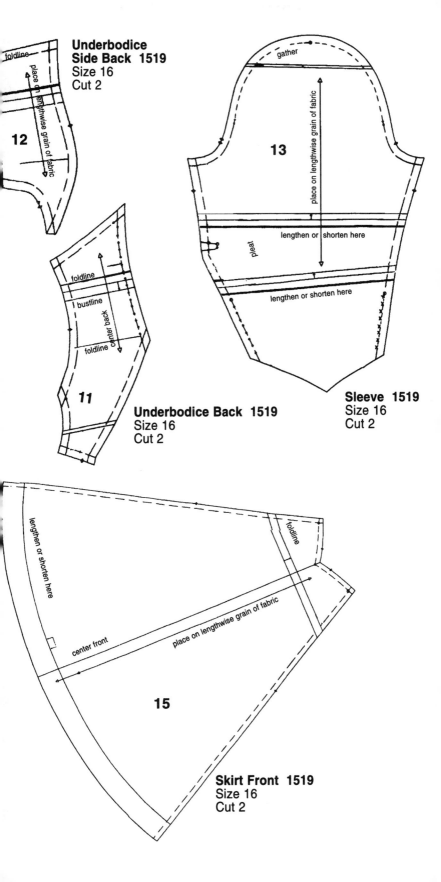

Underbodice Side Back 1519
Size 16
Cut 2

foldline

place on lengthwise grain of fabric

12

Underbodice Back 1519
Size 16
Cut 2

foldline
bustline
foldline
center back

11

gather

place on lengthwise grain of fabric

13

lengthen or shorten here

pleat

lengthen or shorten here

Sleeve 1519
Size 16
Cut 2

lengthen or shorten here

foldline

center front

place on lengthwise grain of fabric

15

Skirt Front 1519
Size 16
Cut 2

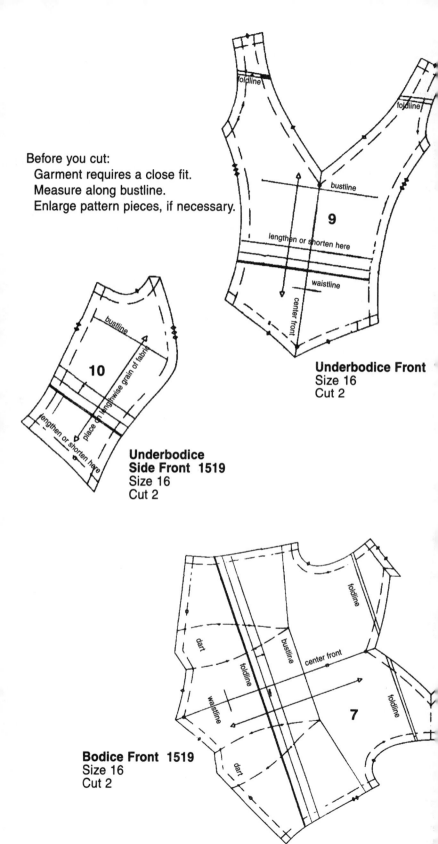

Before you cut:
  Garment requires a close fit.
  Measure along bustline.
  Enlarge pattern pieces, if necessary.

foldline

foldline

foldline

bustline

9

lengthen or shorten here

waistline

center front

Underbodice Front
Size 16
Cut 2

bustline

10

place on lengthwise grain of fabric

lengthen or shorten here

**Underbodice
Side Front 1519**
Size 16
Cut 2

foldline

dart

bustline

foldline

center front

waistline

foldline

7

dart

Bodice Front 1519
Size 16
Cut 2

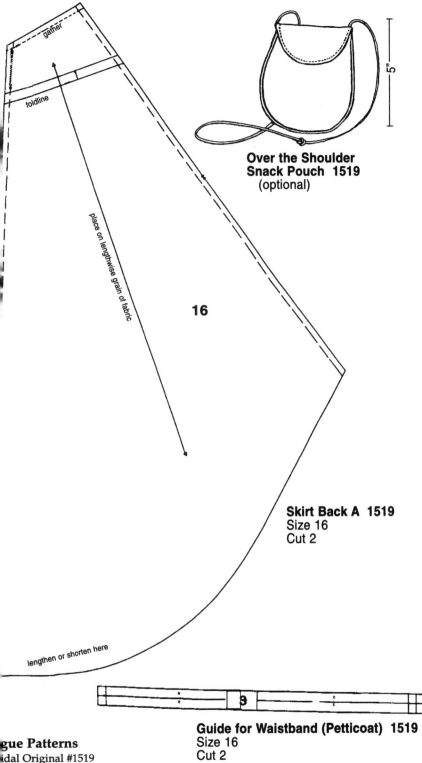

gather

foldline

place on lengthwise grain of fabric

16

**Over the Shoulder
Snack Pouch 1519**
(optional)

5"

Skirt Back A 1519
Size 16
Cut 2

lengthen or shorten here

3

Guide for Waistband (Petticoat) 1519
Size 16
Cut 2

gue Patterns
idal Original #1519
gue Pattern Service
1 Avenue of the Americas
:w York, New York 10013
utterick Company, Inc., 1985